MG CARS
1930 to 2006
A Pictorial History
Trevor Alder

First published in 2025 by Veloce, an imprint of David and Charles Limited. Tel +44 (0)1305 260068 / e-mail info@veloce.co.uk / web www.veloce.co.uk.
ISBN: 9781836440048 British Library Cataloguing in Publication Data – A catalogue record for this book is available from the British Library. Design and production by Veloce. Printed and bound in the UK by Short Run Press Ltd.

MG CARS

1930 to 2006

A Pictorial History

Trevor Alder

CONTENTS

INTRODUCTION

The MG Car Company was formed in the late 1920s, emerging out of Morris Garages of Oxford, which had previously offered a number of tuned Morris cars, and advertised them in the national press. This book picks up the MG car story from the 1930s until the Rover group collapsed in 2005. All mainstream models are represented, with references to those models that also became available for overseas markets.

Throughout the chapters, in blue boxes, are a variety of the headlines and slogans used in contemporary advertising from various sources, including some from overseas, particularly the USA. These are certainly not exhaustive (there truly are hundreds for certain models) but I have tried to include every model manufactured where possible. One or two of the adverts would probably not make it past the censors today, and many have been forgotten, but some of them are shown within this volume.

The book is divided into logical chapters, and within these are included specific model histories, key (but not all) production changes, a brief overview of specifications, performance and a whole variety of photographs, many of them period, that hopefully serve as a useful guide. The latest overseas built models are not included.

Thanks to Brown & Gammons MG dealership for its impromptu hospitality (see picture below) and to the many keen owners and enthusiasts I have spoken to at various locations, including many classic car gatherings in Suffolk. The British Motor Museum at Gaydon is certainly worth a visit too, with a number of very interesting exhibits, both cars and trucks. If you are interested in local Abingdon history, you should visit the very friendly free museum in the centre of town, where you will also discover one of the last MGB roadsters built.

Just remember, if you drive an MG … "Your mother wouldn't like it," as pointed out in those early 1970s UK advertisements of loud styles, colours and flared trousers!

Trevor Alder
Ipswich, UK

The Abingdon factory closed on 24th October 1980. Auctioneers sold the remaining contents in March 1981, a sad day for MG enthusiasts. Items sold included:

- *The boardroom table – £747*
- *The octagonal boardroom clock – £172*
- *Boardroom sideboard – £230*
- *Eight firemen's helmets – £138 to £195*

The author visiting the very helpful MG dealership Brown & Gammons, at Baldock, Hertfordshire.

1930-1939 – EARLY SPORTS CARS AND BIG EARLY SALOONS

The Six, 18/80 models

The 18/80 was the first mainstream model produced after the MG Car Company was formed. It was born out of the abortive Morris Light Six of 1927, and was produced as a saloon, a few coupés plus two- and four-seater open cars.

Manufactured from 1928 to a very high standard, these comfortable cars were somewhat restricted in width inside, the external body being just 5ft 1in wide. Notwithstanding, a wider track was used on the Mk2 from 1929 that allowed for at least some more passenger space, and revisions were made to the final drive ratio (up to 4.27:1 from 4.25:1). Mk2 cars had revised rocker cover breathers, remote extension to the gear lever and a four-speed gearbox (with 'silent-third') superseded the three-speeds of the Mk1.

"One is so impressed with the ease of gear changing, and that very silent 'third' that one changes gear for the sheer fun of it, snicking into 'second' quite unnecessarily to round street corners and dropping into 'third' when one wishes to overtake another vehicle." This was a quote from *Motor* when its Mk2 was track tested at 78mph at the Brookland track facility, after an initial 2000 miles of 'running in'. Unusually Mk1 and Mk2 production overlapped. There were approximately 500 Mk1s built and 236 Mk2s.

A Speed model was produced from 1930, based on the Mk1 but with a Dewandre servo assisted braking system. In the same year, just five road-racing 18/100 Six (Mk3) models were produced, the all-flying model of the day. This model, known as the Tigress, utilised a tuned version of the 2468cc engine that was shared by all six models. Twin dampers were provided at the rear, a bigger fuel tank, better brakes and lowered suspension. 110mph was entirely possible where roads allowed.

BODY TYPES 'SIX' 18/80: Saloon and coupé four-seater; **manufactured at:** Abingdon; **approximate number produced:** 741;

18/80s standing at the old factory.

Magna 18/80.

Six Tourer of 1929.

production span; 1928-1933.
PERFORMANCE: Top speed: 78mph/125km/h; **average economy:** 18mpg.
PRICE AT LAUNCH: £525 (Mk1), £625 (Mk2).
MEASUREMENTS: Length: 13ft 9in (3.58m); **width:** 5ft 1in (1.55m); **height:** 5ft 6in (1.67m); **wheelbase:** 9ft 6in (2.9m); **kerb weight:** 23cwt (1169kg); **wheels:** 28/29in; **turning circle:** 43ft 0in (13.1m); **fuel capacity**: 12 gallons/54.5 litres.
TECHNICAL: Engine types: 2468cc six-

1929 M-Type Midget.

cylinder petrol; **gearbox:** three- then four-speed; **suspension:** semi-elliptic springs front and rear; **brakes:** drum front and rear.
TRIM: Leather.

Earliest Midgets

M-Type

Enter the MG Midget M-Type 8/33 of 1928. Fitted with very early three-speed gearboxes, these handsome two-seaters charmed the nation with their great looks and addictive character. This was the model that brought sports cars within the reach of the masses, particularly the younger generation, and 3235 units were sold. Power came from the 847cc engine popular with all the Midgets up to 1935. Production took place at Cowley, and the chassis was based on the current Morris Minor of the time, but with lowered suspension. Nearly 40mpg was achievable if driven sensibly, with a top speed of around 60-65mph. Power of the engine was increased from 20 to 27hp in 1930, and the model has been forever popular in club racing. A coupé version, the 'Sportsman', was also produced.

C-Type

Two years later in 1931, the C-Type Midget was revealed. Just 44 of these quirky looking Midgets were produced, all supplied as two-seater sports cars. Known as the Montlhéry Midget, the model succeeded in various motor sport events, the 1931 TT race being notable. Unusual features included the semi-enclosed grille (due to the aerodynamic radiator cowl), pointed tail body, exterior exhaust pipes and twin fold-down wind deflectors for the driver and passenger. To make the car eligible for 750cc motor events, the engine used a shorter stroke than its stablemate Midgets. The engine had a revised crankshaft plus a £345 blown version with an AB head with 52½hp. The braking system could be adjusted from inside the car. A Mk2 version looked more subdued, but the two-seater body still conformed to international racing regulations.

D-Type

The D-Type Midget was also announced in

C-Types at the factory.

D-Type Midget.

1931. Just 250 were produced, this time as a four-seater car in either open or closed form, and still using the little 847cc four-cylinder engine. There were obvious styling differences compared to the M-Type; namely a slightly raked front grille, a reworked body on a longer C-Type chassis and blackened wheel arches. The 84in wheelbase was lengthened by two inches during the short production period (1931-1932).

J-Type – J1

From 1932 to 1933 MG produced the J1 four-seater 'Salonette' or the open car. Again, in open body form, with raiseable fabric hood and the trusty 847cc overhead cam engine, a total of 380 models were built, just 40 percent

J-Type.

of the volume that the J2 attained. This model was built on the D-Type chassis with C-Type mechanicals. Gearboxes were now four-speed with a central remote lever, and twin carburettors were fitted. Cutaway doors were a new feature. Performance details were: 78mph top speed, and 30-50mph acceleration in 10½ seconds in 3rd gear, according to the 1932 *Autocar* road test which stated: "The maximum speed and acceleration figures were taken with the windscreen folded down flat on the scuttle." The open version retailed at £220, and the Salonette at £255.

J2

With a higher production run, the 1932-1934 J2 Midget was more popular than the J1 manufactured alongside it. Perhaps the first of the classic Midgets, this early Midget is identified with pre-swept type wings, suicide doors, and a spare wheel mounted on the rear. Distinctively adopted from this point on were the trade-mark octagonal style instruments which lasted through to the Farina Magnette in the mid-1960s. *Autocar* magazine obtained 82mph with a highly tuned model prepared from the factory, and the story goes that some drivers broke their crankshafts trying to copy the magazine's test driver. Handling, steering and braking were all described as excellent.

J3 and J4

Now commanding high sums – if you can find one – are the two special two-seater sports cars which were produced as J-Types, the J3 and J4. They used the original 746cc Midget engine, although the roadgoing J3 had a Powerplus blower and forged crank, whilst the

A 1932 J-Type Midget.

72hp J4 used an uprated Powerplus blower and a new block plus a counterbalanced crank. Like the previous Montlhéry Midget, external side exhausts were the order of the day, but the car was fitted with a one-piece windscreen this time.

BODY TYPES EARLIEST 'MIDGETS' M-, D-, C- AND J-TYPE: Two-door two-seater open and Sportsman's coupé; **manufactured at:** Abingdon/Cowley; **approximate number produced:** 6023; **production span:** 1929-1934.
PERFORMANCE: Top speed: 65-80mph/105-125km/h; **average economy:** 35-40mpg.
PRICE AT LAUNCH: £175.
MEASUREMENTS: Length: 10ft 4in (3.15m); **width:** 4ft 3¾in (1.33m); **height:** 4ft 4½in (1.34m); **wheelbase:** 6ft 6in then 7ft 2in (1.98 then 2.18m); **kerb weight:** 11cwt (559kg); **wheels:** 17in; **turning circle:** 36ft 0in (11m); **fuel capacity:** 4½ then 12 gallons/20.5 then 55 litres.
TECHNICAL: Engine types: 847cc four-cylinder petrol; **gearbox:** three-speed then four-speed manual; **suspension:** semi-elliptic springs front and rear; **brakes:** drum front and drum rear.
TRIM: Fabric, leather.
KEY OPTIONAL EXTRAS: Four-speed gearbox from 1930.

A PA Midget interior.

PA type headlamp and grille arrangement.

PA Midget engine.

P-Type – PA and PB

Hot on the heels of the J-Type Midgets, around 2000 PA Midgets were produced between 1934 and 1935. Traditional two- and four-seater open cars were produced, as well as the distinctive 'Airline' coupé, all with a slightly longer wheelbase than previously. Many mechanical items were updated, including larger brakes, a stronger clutch and Bishop cam steering. Recessed trafficators were now part of the specification, and the new mechanicals and aerodynamics meant that 75mph was possible, one magazine obtaining 76mph around the Brooklands banked circuit.

Between 1934 and 1935, the PB Midget was manufactured, again with open two- or four-seater bodies and that stylish Airline coupé. The main update here was the adoption of a larger 43hp 939cc engine, and slightly higher ratios on first and second gears making a good car even better. The traditional honeycomb radiator grille was replaced by a vertical slatted version, and speedometer and rev counters were now separate. The straight-through Burgess exhaust gave this Midget a distinctive noise.

BODY TYPES 'MIDGET' PA & PB: Open two-seater and coupé four-seater two-door; **manufactured at:** Abingdon; **approximate number produced:** 2499; **production span:** 1934-1936.
PERFORMANCE: Top speed: 76mph/120km/h; **0-60mph/100km/h:** 27

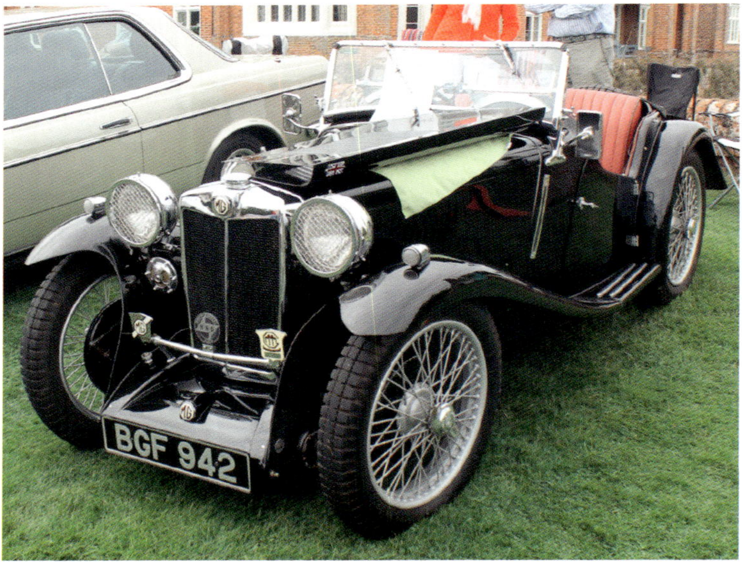

A beautiful PA at Helmingham Hall, Suffolk in 2024.

seconds; **average economy:** 35mpg.
PRICE AT LAUNCH: £222.
MEASUREMENTS: **Length:** 10ft 11in (3.3m); **width:** 4ft 4½in (1.33m); **wheelbase:** 7ft 3½in (2.22m); **kerb weight:** 14cwt (711kg); **wheels:** 19in; **turning circle:** 34ft 0in (10.4m); **fuel capacity**: 12 gallons/54.5 litres.
TECHNICAL: **Engine types:** 847 then 949cc four-cylinder petrol; **gearbox:** four-speed manual; **suspension:** semi-elliptic springs front and rear; **brakes:** drum front and drum rear.
TRIM: Leather.

Magna Six, F-Type and L-Type

The F-Type Magna was produced between October 1931 and 1932, and was sold as either a two-seater or four-seater open car for £250, or a four seater coupé for £289. Production ran to 1250 examples built. Power was by the Wolseley Hornet-based 1271cc six-cylinder engine but with twin carburettors and a short 'remote' gear lever, the 'box being a similar type to be used on the Montlhéry Midget. The tin-top version was the Foursome coupé and came with a sliding roof. Several English coachbuilders built variations including Vanden Plas and a specification change to 12in brake drums was first exhibited at the 1932 Motor Show.

The L-Type Magna followed the F-Type, and was available between 1933 and 1934. The L1 was a four-seater, whilst the L2 used the two-seater configuration and differed from the previous F-Type by way of swept wings, cutaway doors and a flared scuttle. The model was released to the press in

Magna.

1931 F-Type Magna.

Magna 1.5-litre.

September 1933, and they were impressed with the pleasing lines of the L-Type and its long graceful mudguards. There was a large fuel tank at the rear with a gauge visible on the top, and a two-way control for switching to the two-gallon reserve fuel tank. Both cars used the 1087cc six-cylinder power unit from the then current Wolseley Hornet. A four-speed crash gearbox was fitted.

Launched at the London Motor Show in late 1933, hardly any of the Continental Coupé types sold, despite a favourable road test in *Autocar* in April 1934. Its reviewer wrote an overview titled: "Very comfortable, beautifully finished small quality car which easily makes high averages". The total production of L-Type Magnas was 486 L1s, and 90 L2s.

BODY TYPES 'MAGNA' F- AND L-TYPE: Open two- and four-seater plus coupé; manufactured at Abingdon; **approximate number produced:** 1826; **production span:** 1931-1934.
PERFORMANCE: Top speed: Varies per model; **0-60mph/100km/h:** 24 seconds; **average economy:** 25mpg.
PRICE AT LAUNCH: £250-£345 model dependent.
MEASUREMENTS: Length: 10ft 4¼in (3.15m); **width:** 4ft 3in (1.3m); **height:** 4ft 2in (1.2794m); **wheelbase:** 7ft 10in (2.39m); **kerb weight:** 19cwt (965kg); **wheels:** 19in (0.48m); **turning circle:** 32ft 6in (9.9m); **fuel capacity**: 6 and 10 gallons/27 and 45 litres.
TECHNICAL: Engine types: 1270 and 1086cc six-cylinder petrol; **gearbox:** four-speed manual; **suspension:** semi-elliptic springs front and rear; **brakes:** drum front and drum rear.
TRIM: Leather.

Magnette, K-Type

The Magnettes were available in saloon form plus an open two- or four-seater. The first ones, the KA and KBs (1932 to mid-1933), were fitted with a 38hp 1087cc six-cylinder engine, whilst the later KD (mid-1933 to early 1934) had the larger 48hp 1271cc six-cylinder engine. The distinction between the KA and KB was that the KA was fitted with a Wilson type preselector (ie, no clutch and described at the time as 'a self-changing gearbox'), and with triple carburettors, while the KB was produced with a manual dry clutch, a crash gearbox and twin carburettors. The model designation for the two-seater was K2.

Just 33 of the special supercharged K3 Magnette were produced from 1933, and it proved to be a successful racer. The 1087cc 105-125hp engines were machined, and the crank was balanced. A No9 Powerplus blower was fitted onboard and driven from the crankcase front via a reduction gear. The later 1934 models had a pointed tail containing a very large 27½ gallon fuel tank for extra time on the track, and a Marshall supercharger. Comprehensive instrumentation included a 6in diameter Jaeger tachometer.

K-Type Magnette of 1932.

The KN Magnette (1933-1934) was a six-cylinder (N-Type) 56hp 1271cc engine two-door car. The chassis came from the long wheelbase K1. The body included a sun roof, sliding windows and a spare wheel was fitted across the rear panel. Over 400 units were manufactured in two wheelbase lengths, for the shorter model there were two-seater sports and two versions of the K3, a racing model, one of which was supercharged.

The 72mph N Magnette production ran from 1934 to 1936, the car being an open two- or four-seater two-door tourer with a handful of Airline coupés produced. The same 1271cc six-cylinder engine powered this model and produced 56hp as fitted. Effectively four N-Type Magnettes were produced: NA, NB, ND and the works sports racer, the 74hp NE built for the 1934 TT race of which just six were produced. All were fitted with a four-speed manual gearbox. 745 NBs were produced and it was described in its day as a delightful car to handle.

BODY TYPES 'MAGNETTE' K-TYPE: Saloon, open and sports; **manufactured at:** Abingdon; **approximate number produced:** 1351; **production span:** 1932-1936.
PERFORMANCE: **Top speed:** 75-80mph/120-125km/h; **0-60mph/100km/h:** 23 seconds; **average economy:** 24mpg.
PRICE AT LAUNCH: £305-£399.
MEASUREMENTS: **Length:** 12ft 6in (3.81m); **width:** 4ft 7in (1.4m); **height:** 5ft in (1.52m); **wheelbase:** 9ft 0in (2.75m); **kerb weight:** 21cwt (1067kg); **wheels:** 19in and 18in; **turning circle:** 38ft 0in (11.6m); **fuel capacity**: 10 gallons/45 litres.
TECHNICAL: **Engine types:** 1086, 1100 and 1287cc six-cylinder petrol; **gearbox:** four-speed manual; **suspension:** semi-elliptic springs front and rear; **brakes:** drum front and rear.
TRIM: Leather.
KEY OPTIONAL EXTRAS: Supercharger £100 extra.

The big saloons: (SA, VA and WA)

The first new model to be announced after the merger with Morris Motors in July 1935, MG moved into the large plush saloon sector in 1936 with the big SA '2-litre' model launched at the previous year's London Motor Show. Some consider the SA to be a successor, after four years, to the previous 18/80 model. Initially advertised as 2062cc, then produced as 2288 and in 1937 2322cc, the six-cylinder engine was borrowed from the Wolseley 18/80 Six. The engine type was eventually actually bigger than the model name suggested.

The 2-litre SA luxury car of 1936.

It took a while for MG to get through the new Morris red tape to get the bigger engines approved, and some customers could not wait six months and ordered different make luxury cars elsewhere that were available from stock. Perhaps like the later Magnettes, the SA was not a true sports car, more a large, heavy (over 30cwt) luxury car with ample performance. Around 2700 were produced at a very reasonable £375 until 1939 when production ceased.

The bonnet line was kept impressively low by using horizontal dashpots on the downdraught carburettors. The upswept styling was very attractive using an entirely new chassis. The SA was long at 16ft 4in, with a 10ft 3in wheelbase. The original four-speed crash gearbox was soon replaced with a 'box with synchro on top gears. Suspension was by all round semi-elliptic springs still at this stage, but they gave the car a very smooth ride. The striking instrument panel was indirectly lit and sloped back at an angle for ease of reading. Instrumentation however was not octagonal.

MG advert copy writers were proud of the luxury interior, complete with central armrest in the back, front bucket seats, rear side windows that could be used as vents and sumptuous use of leather. The contemporary advertising for the SA almost reads as 1950s Jaguar "For space … for grace … for pace …"

The smaller '1½-litre' VA sat on a 9ft 0in wheelbase – it had an overall length of 13ft 1½in, and was powered by a four-cylinder 54hp 1548cc engine, again of Wolseley origin. Options included an open four-seater tourer configuration, a saloon, or a drophead coupé. 2407 were produced of which 1259 were saloons.

Motor magazine performed an extended road test of a 1½-litre tourer in July 1937 and wrote: "… a car with infinite charm and one with a wide appeal". Its drivers attained 77mph with the windshield up, and over 80mph with the screen folded down. "These are very satisfying figures from a car which weighs some 24cwt laden and costs only £280." Zero to 60mph acceleration times recorded were 22.6 seconds, with 70mph following at 37 seconds. Its hood folded and dropped into a recess behind the rear seats. There was no octagonal instrumentation, but the array of switches and gauges was impressive, as was the use of a four-spoke steering wheel.

Upsizing again to the SA-style, big bodied WA '2.6-litre', and beyond, production slid into the end of the 1930s, and just 369 vehicles were produced between 1938 and 1939 when manufacture ceased. These included another open six-cylinder four-seater tourer by Charlesworth (£450, but just nine built), and a saloon type (£442) or Tickford drophead coupé (£468).

The 15ft 11in WA used a bored-out 2561cc engine, of higher compression ratio, that originated from the SA. Brakes were now larger at 14in and hydraulically operated, and the rear axle was wider than the SA which the new vehicle heavily resembled. This was the most luxurious MG to date, with more capacious coachwork, 18in wire wheels, sumptuous leather seats and door panels with thick wood cappings completely surrounding the glass. A wooden dashboard was fitted with a silver finished inlay for the oval instrumentation display. This display included new style octagonal instrumentation with a 100mph speedometer, electric fuel gauge, water temperature, rev counter, oil pressure ammeter gauges, leather seating with rear fold-down armrest. The spare road wheel was mounted alongside the bonnet which gave a much better capacity within the luggage area that housed a very comprehensive tool-kit. Behind the hinged front bumper badge, there was a hole to insert a starting handle. MG was certainly ahead with the electrics; if the headlamps were on, the interior light would illuminate when either one of the rear doors were opened.

The 2.6-litre was the most expensive prewar car in the MG range. The top of the range Folding head Foursome retailed at £468 in late 1938. It was also the last of the six-cylinder models until the postwar MGC evolved 28 years later, and the even later 6R4 Metro rally car.

BODY TYPES '2-LITRE' SA, VA AND WA: Saloon four-door, open and coupé; **manufactured at:** Abingdon; **approximate number produced:** 5514; **production span:** 1936-1939.

PERFORMANCE: Top speed: 80mph/130km/h; **0-60mph/100km/h:** 22 seconds; **average economy:** 24mpg.
PRICE AT LAUNCH: £280-£442 model dependent.
MEASUREMENTS: Length: 16ft 4in (4.98m); **width:** 5ft 6in (1.67m); **wheelbase:** 10ft 3in (3.12m); **kerb weight:** 22cwt (1100kg); **wheels:** 18in and 19in; **turning circle:** 38ft in (11.6m); **fuel capacity**: 12½ and 16 gallons/56 and 72 litres.
TECHNICAL: Engine types: 2062, 2288 and 2322cc (SA), 1546cc (VA) and 2561cc (WA), all six-cylinder petrol; **gearbox:** four-speed manual; **suspension:** semi-elliptic springs front and rear; **brakes:** drum front and drum rear, twin master cylinders on WA.
TRIM: Leather.

All early MGs media advertising slogans

The most beautiful thing on four wheels! (1924 four-seater Morris)
Britain's Brightest Bay Car! (1929 Midget)
Road holding at Sixty! (8/33 Midget, 1929)
The fascination of the Midget (8/33)
For beautiful bodies on the famous Morris chassis
Ideal sports car!
As chalk from cheese! (1932 Magna)
A product of enthusiasm (1930 Midget)
Featherweight fabric sports saloon (Mark IV)
Britain's most popular sports car
Lord of the open road
A true thoroughbred – perfected by successful racing experience (N Type)
Definitely the fastest (1935 Magnette)
It passes, it surpasses
The supreme British sports car (Midget, Magna & Six, 1931)
For space … for grace … for pace … (2-litre SA)

T-SERIES MIDGETS

The T-Series of Midgets were produced between 1936 and 1954, spanning two periods of pre and then postwar motoring. The name Midget was a continuation of MG's two-seater budget sports cars produced since 1928, and had previously been used on the M-Type, C-Type, D-Type, J-Type, P-Type, and racing Q-Type (as covered in the motor sport section of this book).

The TA was built from mid-1936, TB just in 1939 alone, TC from late 1945, TD from late 1949, and TF from late 1953 until 1955, with each type designation replacing the earlier one. There was no TE type Midget ever produced, for fear, as the legend has it, it may be referred to, laughably, as the 'Tee Hee' car. All models had an engine capacity of around 1.2 litres, except for the late TFs at 1500cc.

Above and below, a 1936 Midget dashboard.

TA Midget

The TA series Midget was the first MG built after Abingdon had lost its independent design office, which was rehoused at Cowley. The Nuffield Organisation had sold the MG Car Company to Morris Motors. The powers that be had instructed Cecil Kimber and his team to return to greater profits, and MG's racing programme stopped abruptly.

The new, larger TA Midget used a bigger Morris 10 pushrod 1292cc long stroke engine with twin SU carburettors, nothing like the previous Midget engines, and the model proved more comfortable than the earlier P-Types. There was better weatherproofing for long distance touring. Built on an ash wood frame, the bodywork was of traditional construction, and Lockheed hydraulic brakes were fitted. A large 15-gallon fuel tank was placed at the rear, three gallons of which was a reserve that could be used by way of a dashboard-mounted two-way switch; no more dangerous fuel cans in the boot, or long glances at the gauge eking out every last drop. A lot of work had been performed to achieve a less polluted ride, with engine fumes breathing through a pipe into the air

Above: Midget with spare wheel mounted on the rear. Right: 1936 Midget radiator cap.

cleaners, and a crankcase that was vented under the vehicle. 19in wire wheels were the order of the day with centre locks. The four-speed manual gearbox was uprated with synchromesh in third and top gears in August of 1936, when a remote gear changer was fitted along with modifications to the gear ratios. The clutch was of a cork insert type. Unusually, despite the seat squabs having separate cushions, the back rest was common to driver and passenger and it was adjustable for rake. The front grille colour matched the car's upholstery, which was a nice touch.

When launched, the adverts read: "MG make a Midget Series 'T'. Bigger – and quite a bit better. 10hp now! Speed, acceleration, braking, road-holding – all proportionately better too. An exciting car this ...". Around 3000 TAs were manufactured, with just under ten percent having the attractive Tickford drophead bodywork.

TB Midget

Introduced with the TB Midget was a 1250cc four-cylinder XPAG engine of 54hp, being a bored out version of the Morris Ten 1140cc unit. Production started in early 1939 and lasted just four months until the outbreak of war. Production ceased in October 1939 and the Abingdon factory was cleared out to prepare for munitions manufacturing.

The XPAG engine had a larger bore and shorter stroke than the previous unit, and secured a considerable increase in power. The engine was used through to the earliest of the TF cars.

A very original TB centre dash.

A beefier Borg & Beck clutch with single dry plate was standardised in place of the earlier oil-bath cork type. Synchromesh was available on the top three gears, and there was now a lower ratio back axle and a telescopic steering column. Hydraulic shock absorbers were fitted front and rear and the rear axle used sliding trunnions (instead of shackles) to prevent any side play.

Just 379 TBs were built. The heavier Tickford dropheads, conveniently with separate bucket seats on sliding runners, wind-up windows and increased passenger and luggage area, accounted for 60 of these. Salmon bodies on the TB were available, all in for £270 delivered. Outwardly the TB was very similar to its forebear, but could quickly be identified by the creased rear wing (a design carried forward after the war for the TC), different cooling louvres on each side of the engine, and centre-laced wire wheels (the TAs were side laced). The larger fuel tank could easily propel the car for up to 500 miles – if you could fill it, as fuel was now in very short supply due to wartime restrictions.

Front aspect of a TB, in rarely produced optional silver metallic paint. Owner Clive Sheriff has had this car for 60 years.

Left and above: A TC Midget, with spare wheel mounted on the rear.

TC Midget

After a six year break, a government-promoted export drive commenced for all UK car companies. In addition there was a general shortage of steel, with many manufacturers turning to other metals. Many of the TCs built from October 1945 went to the USA. The TC was nearly identical to the TB but had a 2in wider body and the use of conventional spring shackles all round.

It is estimated that 10,000 TCs were built, all in right-hand drive, making them an excellent choice to bring back from dry overseas markets in later years. Attributes such as a steering wheel that could adjust up and down, plus forwards and backwards, were very welcome on a car of this modest price.

In a 1947 road test of the TC, *Autocar* commented: "One quickly comes to feel an affection for its efficiency and willingness,

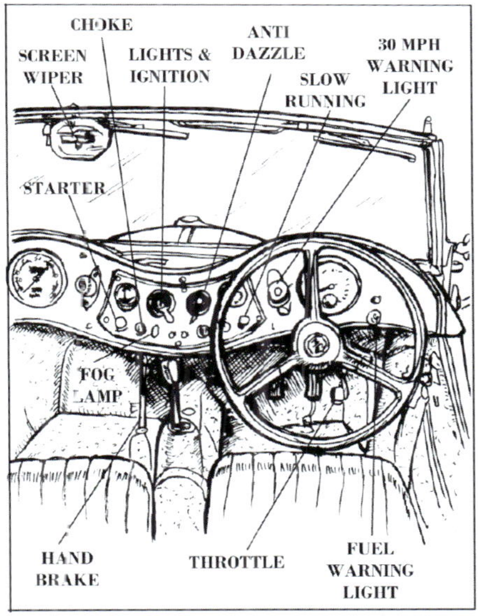

Above: TC Midget dashboard layout.

The TC Midget was manufactured until 1949.

This TC Midget has been beautifully restored. A cream MG badge and radiator cap can be seen on the front.

An early 1970s US advert featuring a TC Midget alongside the MGB.

and in all respects, including performance, it is 'man-size', with no suggestions of the tiny car about it". The magazine recorded an average touring petrol consumption of 28-34 mpg, a top speed of 75mph and 0-60mph acceleration time of 22.7 sec. The TC was Abingdon's last beam-axle car.

TD Midget

November 1949 saw the introduction of the TD Midget, and this became the highest selling and arguably most popular Midget, with 29,664 units produced. It had the same running gear and basic style lines as the TC, but the recently launched YA 1¼-litre saloon model lent its chassis configuration to the TD. Thus the TD was equipped with coil spring front suspension and 'direct-action' rack and pinion steering. The steering was now a lot lighter, and with a better steering lock. Full chrome bumpers were fitted with over-riders and a tuned variant was available from May 1950. Wheel size was reduced to 15in, but these came as steel 'disc' versions only. No wire wheels were fitted, however many have been retrofitted since. From new, the wheels had wider tyres fitted than the TC. The dashboard reverted to round 5in dials. Overall contemporary tests show that the TD has very similar performance figures to its forebear the TC.

The expensive Arnolt TD Bertone coupé was a very tidy looking conversion available

Early brochure for the TD Midget.

Press photograph of the TD Midget.

on the North American market, with no resemblance at all to the Abingdon car. Chassis were delivered to the Turin facility in small batches direct from the factory, with an MG guarantee plate bolted to the metalwork and a full dashboard with instrumentation. The bodywork was part steel, part aluminium, with the main body frames welded to the chassis. The interiors of the Arnolt TD Bertone coupé were very highly trimmed, and at first glance could pass as an expensive 1950s piece, of Italian origin. A convertible version based on the new body lines, was also offered, as were supercharged versions. Door windows were of wind-up type, and the side glass in the rear opened out like the MGB. Production continued right through the 1950s, with perhaps 100 being built in total at a selling price of about $5000 each.

TD dashboard.

TF Midget

It had been intended that the 1955 MGA would replace the now older looking Midgets, but the idea was vetoed by BMC bosses. With the advent of the new Austin-Healey 100, sales of the Midgets were dropping and the MGA would not be available for two years, so a stop gap was needed. An enthusiastic public were shown the debut of the TF at the London Motor Show in 1953 and admired its rakish lines, lower bonnet and slightly curved grille. "The enthusiast's car, designed for the sheer joy of driving" stated the full page adverts in the press.

This more modern looking Midget was based on the 7ft 10in wheelbase, as used in the previous Midgets, but the TF had restyled wings, a front end with fixed rather than openable sides to the bonnet. That striking new front grille and the headlamps were lowered a little and featured their own housing.

TD grille and headlamps.

TD Midget on the production line at Abingdon.

This housing was now neatly amalgamated into the front wings. Wire wheels were again offered, and were fitted to around two thirds of the cars from new. Inside there was new style (back again to octagonal) instrumentation, and a completely revised dashboard. Windscreens made of safety glass could still be folded flat onto the bonnet scuttle panel.

Halfway through production in September 1954, the XPEG engine, bored-out to 1466cc and producing 63hp, replaced the smaller XPAG unit which produced 57hp. 9600 TFs were built, 3400 being the last 1.5-litre models before production stopped in early 1955 to make way for the new, more aerodynamic MGA.

One or two police forces took deliveries of the TF including that in Kent; the author wonders if it became the rule to remove the flat police hat before driving at speed with the roof down! Sadly, none of the UK weeklies or monthly *Motor Sport* magazine performed a full road test of the TF, concentrating on the Magnette if an MG test car was made available. Ironically, *Classic & Sportscar* magazine tested a TF in a twin test with the Naylor mentioned below, some 30 years later in 1985

T-SERIES MIDGET BODY TYPE (ALL MODELS): Two-door roadster; **manufactured at** Abingdon; **approximate number produced:** 52,646; **production span:** 1936-1954.
PERFORMANCE: Top speed: 78mph/125kph; **0-60mph/100kph:** 23 seconds; **average economy:** 27mpg.
PRICE AT LAUNCH: £222.
MEASUREMENTS: Length: TA 11ft 7¼in (3.53m), TB and TC 12ft 1in (3.68m), TD 12ft 3in (3.73m), TF 12ft 3in (3.73m); **width:** 4ft 8in (1.42m) TA, TB and TC, 4ft 11in (1.5m) TD and TF; **height:** 4ft 5in (1.33m) TA, TB and TC, 4ft 6in (1.37m) TD and TF; **wheelbase:** 7ft 10in (2.38m) all models; **kerb weight:** 1995lb (904kg); **wheels:** 19in TA, TB and TC, 15in TD and TF; **turning circle:** 38ft 0in (11.6m) TA, TB and TC, 31ft TD and TF; **fuel capacity:** 10½-12 gallons plus three gallon reserve/47-55 litres plus 13-litre reserve (varies).

Left: The TF Midget engine. Below: TFs reverted to the octagonal instruments.

TECHNICAL: Engine types: 1292, 1250 then 1466cc four-cylinder petrol; **gearbox:** four-speed manual; **suspension:** semi-elliptic leaf springs front and rear TA, TB and TC, then coils at front (TD and TF); **brakes:** drums with Lockheed hydraulic foot brake, independent cable operated handbrake.
TRIM: Leather.

Other T-series Midget-like projects

NCG Design of New Milton offered its kit car solution to the TA and TC, building them at the rate of one per week in the early 1980s. This concept was based on existing second-hand MGB running gear and would accept the MGB V8 engine as a donor, if anybody was breaking one. Essex-based Merlin produced a lookalike Cortina-kit car in 1983 which was a glass-fibre body mounted over a tubular steel chassis.

The following year, the Yorkshire-built Naylor TF, the design of which was based heavily on the Midget TF, was fully EC type approved, even for a low production run. It was fitted out with Connolly leather seats, beautiful carpets and genuine spoked wheels. The theme of octagonal instrumentation was not carried over. Partly developed by BL, it was sold through official Leyland dealers and competed heavily with the similar priced Morgan cars of similar appeal. An ash-wood body frame housed metal body panels and a steel chassis, and the mechanics came from the O-series Morris Marina/Ital Austin Ambassador, with a 1695cc engine producing 77hp. Just over 100 cars were built before Naylor went bust in 1986. The Hutson Motor company took over production and another 60 or so cars (Hutson and Mahcon TF1700) were produced between 1988-1991.

In the early 1980s, over in Rochester, USA, the TF1800 was produced based on an MGB platform as a kit car. Called the Victor Antique Auto TF1800, it was a faithful reproduction but made in glass-fibre and carefully bonded to an ash wood frame. The dimensions of the TF body copy matched the MGB base and running gear exceptionally well. The Colombo brothers, Mike and Rich, were appalled at the original wiring loom of the TF, and had a brand new loom designed by a computer wiring specialist. The end result was a lighter car than the genuine TF, and a faster one. Total cost was $7475 for the kit and $16,500 for a complete car.

Midget TA, TB, TC, TD, and TF media advertising slogans

The new MG Midget is a real sports car
A new MG Midget makes its bow … called Series T (1936 TA)
In fact a faster, finer sports car altogether (TA)
The classic MG-TC, the sports car that started it all (USA)
Maintaining the breed (TC)
Possession with personality (TC)
The new TD Midget. With the plus features
New plus features have made it Britain's most talked about sports car
I'll meet you on the MG stand (TD)
Character in every line (TD)
You'd never think this was a bumpy road! (TD)
Touch the throttle and up she goes! (TD)
She's a joy to handle in traffic (TD)
You'll find she's quite roomy for a little 'un (TD)
Safety fast! (TF)
The sports car with winning ways (TF)
The enthusiast's car (TF)
Pretty as a picture (TF)
Meet your MG at the Motor Show (TF & Magnette)

Y-TYPE
"A Refined Fast Touring Car"

As in all cases with elderly cars, the model name referred to, in this case Y-Type (YA and YB), is not the name used on the boot-lid or sales information. This section refers to the MG One and a Quarter Litre saloon model, produced between 1947 and 1953. Production would probably have started in 1941 had there been no Second World War. Some of the bodywork was based on a revised series E Morris 8, again with the 'suicide doors', and the chassis was a longer version of the TD Midget, with the same steering and suspension set up. The car had a reworked front end featuring the very distinctive vertical MG radiator grille. Fuel was fed through an electric petrol pump to a single SU carburettor with a light alloy intake duct coupled to the air cleaner.

The rather narrow frontal interior gave restrictions for drivers with large feet, but was remarkably well populated with interesting features. These included a driver-operated modesty blind for the rear screen, and fully adjustable (fore and aft) front bucket-style designed seats, made to avoid side sway during 'entertaining' driving. The rear seat, really only wide enough for two occupants, was finished with a centrally mounted arm rest. The wooden finished dashboard components included two traditionally styled octagonal dials, but no rev counter. The instrumentation included a speedometer, clock, fuel gauge, oil pressure gauge and ammeter. Neat push-pull switches operated the starter motor, standard fitment fog lamp, dashboard lights, head and side lights. A time delay traffic signal switch was fitted to the steering wheel. The wood cappings were extended to the top of the door cards, and the quite shallow windscreen still opened for added ventilation, like those of prewar cars, achieved by turning a handle on the centre of the dash. A sliding sunroof was a handy addition.

Unlike cheaper cars of the time, twin sun visors were fitted at the top of the screen. Unusually, the steering column was adjustable. The 26in deep rear boot housed the spare wheel and tools in a bottom section behind the number plate, sadly no cubic capacity measurements could be found when researching this book for the luggage area. However, it was found that the boot could accommodate a large suitcase, spare fuel can and miscellaneous packages with the lid still shut. The bootlid had a fold-down miniature tailgate and, when deployed, it provided accommodation for objects nearly 4ft long. The widest part of the modest interior was the leading edge of the rear seat squab, which gave 4ft 10in of usable space, being 9in wider than the same squab point at the front.

YA model 1¼-litre advertising.

Overall the car's external width remained the same at 4ft 11in, the front losing width inside due to the ever widening running boards. The jacking point controller was under the bonnet, the car raised by waggling the lever, with separate and permanent Smiths Jackall jacks below. There were no more inconvenient and time-consuming centre lock hubs, as in days gone by!

The vehicle was aimed at "fathers who've retained their youthful craving for sports motoring" and it was "a handsome and smooth mannered car in town, and a real devil for speed in the open" according to the Abingdon media team in 1947. Those fathers would have to justify paying out an extra £300

YA advertising again, also shown is the tourer version and Midget.

Above: A 1952 1¼-litre saloon advert.
Below: A 1953 1¼-litre saloon advert.

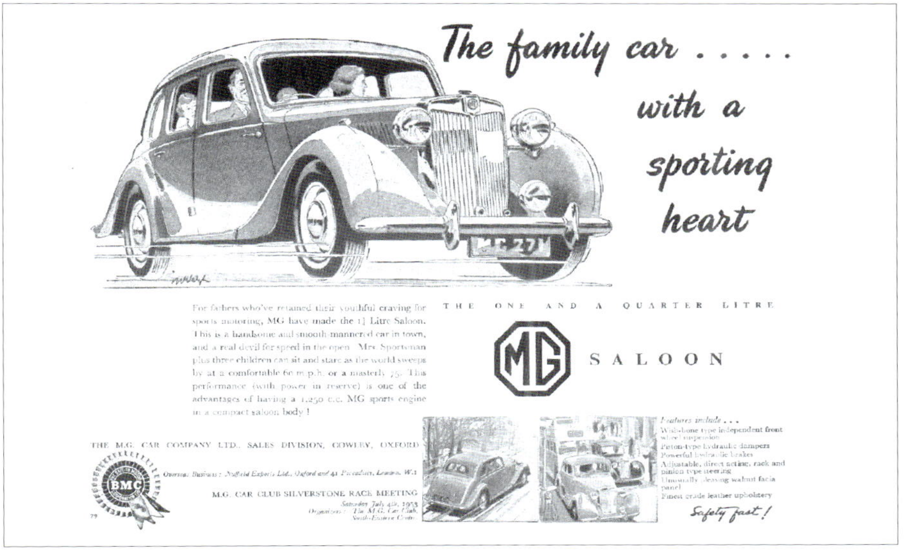

(nearly double) over the price of the smaller-engined similar looking Morris 8 (four-door version) in 1947. Certainly the Y-type could not be accused of concessions to contemporary transatlantic styling trends.

Road testing of the new model, the only four-door MG saloon available for seven years, was keenly performed by the mainstream press. In 1947, *Motor* magazine had early use of a pre-production car that covered 700 miles in the UK, then went on to Ostend via boat, covering another 1000

A 1952 YB 1¼-litre saloon in 2024. Note suicide doors, correct steel wheels, and the handles of the rear-hinged front doors.

miles on the Continent. These days it looks to have unremarkable performance, the 4ft 10in high car could only just achieve 70mph from its 1250cc four-cylinder 11hp engine, but the journalists at the time remarked of a well-known European straight road section "...a speed of 70mph was held at the end of the trip at Jabbeke, a speed actually above the normal maximum, without the car showing any signs of distress."

Other established magazines also had free usage of demonstration models from Abingdon, *Autocar* reporting extensively on its French/Italian road trip, including the difficulties in buying fuel in Italy (they took two jerry cans in case of problems), where books of 50 litres could be bought for £2 sterling, up to a maximum of 300 litres. The only other issues reported were that the Y-type had a thirst for coolant water when pushed (it didn't overheat, however), and consumed battery water due to constant high speed charging. They concluded: "To sum up concerning this nice little car, it is mysterious how it achieves such a speedy performance with an engine the same size as the well-known TC MG Midget but with one carburettor in place of two and about 5cwt more weight." A few months later in 1948, the magazine was driving the same car, DRX557, in the Welsh hills for another travel article.

Production continued for five years, and another model was offered to the press in the spring of 1952, *Autocar* magazine reporting that "the well-equipped model was very pleasing and had an air of a thoroughbred, brought about no doubt by its sporting ancestors".

Production continued until 1953 after 6158 YA cars were built, followed by 1201 YBs. Some 377 YT four-seater, two-door tourers were manufactured between 1948 and 1950, finished in the same colours as the MG TC Midgets: Regency Red, Black, Clipper Blue, Sequoia Cream and Shires Green. The body was supplied, painted and trimmed by Morris Bodies Branch. At Abingdon, the body would be matched and mounted onto a rolling chassis and then fully assembled. Wire wheels were never fitted, the steel wheels supplied with the car were an inch smaller on the YB models, and only finished in Sequoia Cream. Although most of these cars went for export, some have returned, and make the occasional appearance at classic car shows in the UK.

YA, YB, YT BODY TYPES: Four-door saloon and open tourer; **manufactured at:** Abingdon; **approximate number produced:** 7359; **production span:** 1947-1953.
PERFORMANCE: Top speed: 70mph/110km/h; **0-60mph/100km/h:** 27 seconds; **average economy:** 27mpg.
PRICE AT LAUNCH: £671 11s 8d.
MEASUREMENTS: Length: 13ft 5in (4.09m); **height:** 4ft 10in (1.47m); **wheelbase:** 8ft 3in (2.51m); **kerb weight:** 2240lb (1016kg); **wheels:** 16in then 15in (YB); **turning circle:** 35ft 0in (10.67m); **fuel capacity:** 8 gallons/ 36 litres; **boot capacity:** small, with spare wheel mounted below.
TECHNICAL: Engine types: 1250cc four-cylinder petrol; **gearbox:** four-speed manual; **suspension:** (front) independent coil springs with wishbones, (rear) live axle, semi-elliptical leaf springs; **brakes:** hydraulic drum front and drum rear.
TRIM: Leather.
KEY OPTIONAL EXTRAS: HMV Radio, Heater, Duotone paint.

1¼-litre YA & YB media advertising slogans

Maintaining the breed
Versatility
In Leicestershire or Leicester Square
Dual personality; for those who are men about town and boys about speed ...
For sporting men
Combining family-car comfort with celebrated MG sporting performance
The family car ... with a sporting heart

MG MAGNETTE, ZA AND ZB

Designer Gerald Palmer had caught the eye of the Nuffield company bosses back in the late 1940s, having designed the attractive curved body Jowett Javelin shortly before. He was approached and asked to design a new, sleek, larger than average saloon, derivatives of which would be produced with MG, Riley and Wolseley badging. The end result was the ZA MG Magnette which was the smaller of the two similar shells designed and shared with the bigger Riley.

The ZA Magnette resembled the Wolseley 4/44 saloon quite a bit as it shared many body components. However, the bonnet, grille (now curved vertically), wings, and sills were different, giving it a more pronounced appearance – more Italian looking than American, such as its competitors the Vauxhall Velox and Cresta. The radiator cowl and octagonal filler cap were dummies, which lifted with the rear-hinged bonnet to reveal the real radiator filler cap beneath. The all steel monocoque chassis/body was produced by Pressed Steel. Whilst the Wolseley was launched with the earlier but revised XPAG 1250cc engine from the T- and Y-series, the Magnette launch was delayed by a year or so as progress could be made fitting a new British Motor Corporation mid-size engine, following company rationalisation. There were three brand new engines: the 950cc A series, the 1489cc B-series fitted to the new Magnette, and the 2.6-litre six-cylinder C-series for larger cars.

Whilst the crowds were inspecting the new MG TF Midget at its debut at the seemingly traditional London Motor Show in October

An early ZA Magnette.

Early ZA Magnette advertising.

1953, alongside it was shown the new ZA style MG Magnette. The name horrified some MG fanatics, as it had previously been used on MG sports cars (with a rare exception), and here was a fully modern four-door saloon. It was a direct replacement to the earlier One-and-a-Quarter model. Here then was a fresh full-width design (no running boards or separate headlamps, but sadly no sliding roof either) that immediately took MG into the new postwar age. No more so called 'suicide doors' or wind out front windscreen, the comparatively powerful 1489cc 60hp engine could attain 86mph on two-way test run averages, with a 0-60mph acceleration time of around 18.5 seconds. Fuel consumption was a creditable 25mpg overall, with the vehicle weighing in at just over 2400lb.

Advertising was common in the media, which concentrated on how pleasing the car was as a family saloon: "Spirited performance for me ..." the tweed jacketed, pipe smoking chap said, whilst his wife commented "Elegance and comfort for me," a good example of mid-1950s model exposure.

Above: An early ZA Magnette at a Suffolk car show in 2024. Right: ZA rear lamps.

Long gone are the days we read "And for her, everything a woman looks for in a car!"

With its extra width, the wider Magnette could now appeal to families of six, as three could comfortably sit on the two wider front seats, and the sports car style short remote-control gear lever was hardly in the way. The similar Wolseley version had the advantage of having a column gearchange and bench seat which made front seat occupation even easier.

The traditional polished wood veneer dashboard continued, a half octagonal speedometer (with trip recorder) sat in front of the driver, and a Jaeger clock was mounted high up above the anti-glare dipping rear-view mirror – at least now the rear passengers could also see it. Not being an open car, a heater and demister were fitted as standard. Carpets were of ample pile type, and there was a creditable number of trim and colour options available. Available colours included Black, Green, Grey, Maroon, and then from 1955, Steel Blue, Island Green, Birch Grey or Royal Tan. Internal trim colours, including the comfortable seating, were Biscuit, Grey, Maroon and Green.

The rear boot was described as "very capacious" and indeed at 38in wide was far roomier than the previous YA or YB types. For the first time the boot was counterbalanced to aid opening with, like the bonnet, torsion bar springs, and was hinged at the top. The spare wheel was now mounted upright on the left-hand side whilst the tool-kit sat in a recess on the right, revealing quite a depth for suitcases and such like. The fuel tank was also resited, now sitting vertically behind the rear seat. At the rear, a reversing lamp was fitted, lamps were set at the bottom of the wings above the bumper line, and overriders were fitted to the bumpers front and rear. A large octagonal MG badge was placed centrally and halfway up the boot panel. Fuel was taken on by opening a flush panel on the uppermost section of the left rear wing.

Various changes were made after the initial production batch in 1953, including a lower drive ratio, (4.3:1 from the later MGA changed to 4.875:1), which improved acceleration. In addition, a visible clue to an

The chrome trim on the ZA models sloped around the wheelarch.

Interior of the same ZA showing octagonal dials.

early car is the non-adoption of quarterlights in the front doors. Indeed, all diagrams and cutaway drawings published by the contemporary press showed an absence of these windows, although the rear quarterlights were evident. Sales picked up quickly proving the old die-hards wrong about the name, and the model outsold any previous MG saloon. Road test reports were initially scarce in the UK media, but within a year of launch most journals were very favourable and the car proved very much faster than the new Wolseley 4/44 with its smaller and somewhat older engine.

As an aid to increase overseas publicity, three factory prepared Magnettes, KJB908, KJB909 and KJB910 were entered into the high profile 1955 Monte Carlo Rally, each with a three man crew. All Magnette crew members were amateurs, and whilst they did finish the event safely following some disagreements with the MG competition manager over what specialist equipment they should be carrying, they were low placed in the final results at 178th, 202th and 237th overall. A few other events that followed, without major success, included the 1955 RAC Rally, and the Tulip Rally in the spring, one car being driven by Pat Moss who sadly crashed after forgetting to drive on the right hand side of the road. Although speedy repairs were made to her car, and it did start the race, it was soon retired after bearing trouble.

A full wooden dashboard replaced the partly painted metal one used up until March 1955. Onto the ZB models, for the 1957 model year, already with more power as this had previously just increased by 8hp to

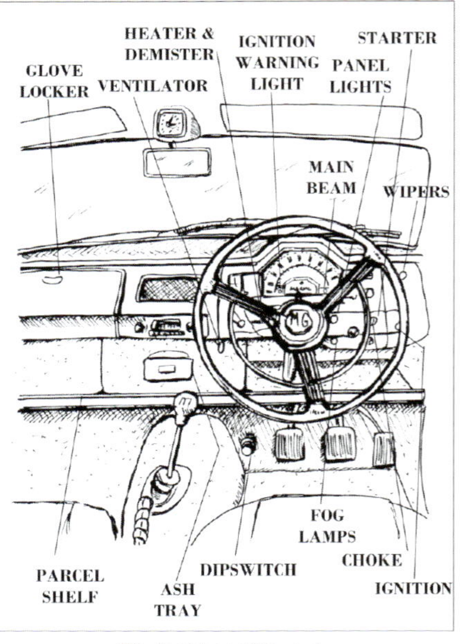

ZA dashboard layout.

68hp a couple of months previously. The power increase was achieved by raising the compression ratio from 7.15 to 8.3, and revisions by gearing up the final drive from 4.9 to 4.55:1. Outwardly the model appeared similar but changes were made to the chromium plated brightwork along the body sides, which no longer took on the distinctive downward curve towards the leading edges of the front wheel arches.

Internally, the facia panel was revised, and a parcel shelf was added underneath. The wider rear screen took on a more pronounced

Side chrome trim differences can be seen here on this ZB, a very tidy example on display at a Suffolk classic car show.

curve and became full width on the very plush looking 'Varitone' models from September 1956. This was years before the Vauxhall Cresta and Velox PA models lost their three-glass piece rear screen in favour of one piece unit. The ZB was available in a wide choice of eight two-tone choices, although confusingly, there was a single colour Varitone model offered too. The paint division was such that that the top colour extended down the top of the rear wings and included the entire boot panel, and up front, the bonnet too. On the sides, the division followed the body crease line, so as to completely encapsulate the window area, which made the whole concept rather attractive. The fussy chromium plated trim pieces were not fitted and there were flashier chrome wheel trims which were often, but not always, fitted.

Some later Magnettes were produced with the less popular selective-automatic Manumatic two-pedal control transmission, also available on Austin A55, Hillman Jubilee Minx, Morris Oxford and Wolseley 15/50. The idea was that the driver could shift gears without the use of the clutch. The scheme proved unpopular, and as the cars became middle aged, and perhaps needed an extra hand to get going, it became evident they could not be push or tow started.

Autocar commented at the end of its 1957 road test of a standard Magnette "As for speed, it is now our fastest native 1½-litre four door saloon, and the basic price of £714 represents a very desirable property." This

Chrome detail at the back of the same ZB.

same sentiment was echoed decades later with the advent of the MG Montego. Thus towards the end of 1958, the last of any Abingdon saloons rolled off the production line. The final retail price was £1072 for the standard car and £1111 for the Varitone version. In all, 36,500 units were built.

All MG badged saloons following this model were manufactured elsewhere, with the launch of the less popular (and not to mention

Rear aspect of the Varitone with wider rear window.

highly badge engineered) Farina shape Magnette in February the following year.

MG ZA ZB MAGNETTE BODY TYPE: Four-door saloon; **manufactured at:** Abingdon; **approximate number produced:** 12,754 (ZA) and 23,846 (ZB), 36,600 of which 7803 Varitone; **production span:** 1953-58.

PERFORMANCE: Top speed: 86mph/ 135km/h; **0-60mph/100km/h:** 18.5 seconds; **average economy:** 26mpg.

PRICE AT LAUNCH: £914 17s 6d.

MEASUREMENTS: Length: 14ft 1in (4.29m); **width:** 5ft 3in (1.6m); **height:** 4ft 10in (1.47m); **wheelbase:** 8ft 6½in (2.6m); **kerb weight:** 2464lb/1118kg; **wheels:** 15in; **turning circle:** 37ft 6in (11.43m); **fuel capacity:** 9½ gallons/43 litres; **boot capacity:** "very capacious".

TECHNICAL: Engine types: 1489cc four-cyl. petrol; **gearbox:** four-speed manual; **suspension:** (front) independent coil springs and wishbones, (rear) live axle semi-elliptic leaf springs with torque arm; **brakes:** drum front and rear.

TRIM: Leather.

KEY OPTIONAL EXTRAS: HMV radio, Manumatic two pedal control (later).

Magnette ZA and ZB media advertising slogans

Safety fast in air-smoothed style (brochure)
Everyone's pleased with the MG Magnette
I have never driven a car with less vice than the Magnette
A lovely car from every angle
Meet your MG at the Motor Show!
Elegance throughout
It brings out the expert in you!
The MG has a magic of its own (with MGA)
For my kind of motoring, it must be an MG
She's driving the car, but the selective manumatic is doing the work!
Magnette & Varitone saloons – Luxury Motoring
Drive a Magnette, it brings out the expert in you!

MGA

In the summer 1955, the Le Mans event saw two MGA prototypes racing, and it had been hoped to launch a new road-going model to the public immediately after; however, this was not the case. Quickly following a secret dealer-only launch hosted at University Motors in London, and similar dealer events in Belgium, Switzerland and New York, a break in MG tradition occurred in September 1955, when the factory publicly announced its new model, but this time at an overseas motor show. Frankfurt was the venue, with a brand new, full road-specification car being transported 450 miles east, last minute, by air to Germany. Back on home turf, from 19 October 1955, an Orient Red MGA accompanied by two Magnettes, appeared on the small MG stand at the Earls Court, London Motor Show. Additionally, a special revolving display was aimed to impress; on one side was an Old English White MGA in left-hand drive with overseas market specification, while a chassis was displayed on the other side, both stacked vertically with a black board between them, enclosed in glass and mounted on a huge round chessboard-style floor.

The MGA was a direct replacement to the (TF) Midget. That name was not adopted for this new model, but of course, in true MG tradition, would later re-emerge in the early 1960s. The shape, although the first MG sports design of a non-traditional type, was not unfamiliar. Three such models, the all-aluminium EX182 prototypes, had been previously entered into the 24 hour Le Mans race that year, two finishing at 12th and 17th overall and at 2087 and 1961 miles driven respectively. This was a commendable finish for a company that had not entered any vehicles in this race for two decades. The last car driven by Dick Jacobs somersaulted and the driver was almost killed, sadly. A fourth EX182 had been used as a practice car. The factory had produced a one-off, EX175 before them, albeit with the smaller 1250cc XPAG engine. Apart from the bonnet bulge needed to clear the earlier engine, the style lines were virtually identical.

The MG 'A' model was all new. A two-door

A 1955 MGA when new.

two-seater roadster for £844 all in including taxes, a £64 raise over its predecessor. It soon became the fastest selling sports car and won hearts around the world. Initially using that 72bhp BMC 1489cc B-series engine with twin carburettors, independent front suspension and, remarkably, to start with, drum brakes all round. At least those brakes proved very good in service. Plain steel wheels with chrome hubcaps were the norm, and centre-lock wire wheels were a popular optional extra. Its wind-cheating body featured a shorter but still curved grille (like the similarly engined Magnette). Twin semi-downdraught 1½in SU carburettors fed fuel to the engine, and maximum torque was produced at 3500rpm, differing from the Le Mans cars. Drive was via a four-speed gearbox (no overdrive, sadly, like the Triumph TR2) with synchromesh on second, third and top gears. Front suspension was identical to the last style used in the Midgets and the Le Mans cars: coil springs with unequal length wishbones. A low

The rear wheel of the MGA was stowed in the shallow boot.

'The Monkees' pop group with their MGA.

A 1959 MGA press advert. Wire wheels were an extra.

centre of gravity negated the use of ant-roll bars. At the rear, half-elliptic springs were fitted, shackled at the rear end controlled by piston type dampers.

The wide aluminium doors were forward hinged, the hinges being concealed within. There were no door handles or locks, access was made by pull cables within the car. The hood was stowed away in an area behind the seats which tipped forwards to allow access where the side screens could also be stowed. An overall tonneau cover was made available at extra cost. The aluminium hinged lid to the very limited rear stowage area was accessible via a catch behind the passenger seat. It was recommended either to place any luggage behind the front seats, or indeed use the boot but leave the spare wheel behind, or mount it on the boot-lid itself. A canvas covered spare wheel lay horizontally on the boot floor, with frankly not a lot of room for much else! The chrome twist-off fuel filler was mounted off-side (UK driver's side) between the right rear light and the lower end of the boot lid. A full width taller windscreen replaced the half-moon Perspex air deflectors seen on the three EX182 racing versions in France.

Interiors were trimmed in leather, with individual bucket-like seats. The new steering wheel, with four-sprung spokes, allowed easy vision of the driver's instruments: A 20mph incremented 4in speedo with headlamp high beam warning lamp within was fitted, plus a similar sized tachometer, which housed the ignition warning lamp. The oil pressure and water temperature gauges were combined. A rheostat-controlled panel lamp was now offered. Dashboards were body coloured (not wood veneer) and an attractive black blanking panel was fitted on the passenger side if the optional radio was not requested.

The 1489cc version of the MGA lasted until 1959. An 'all-weather' metal-top coupé version was soon to be made available in September 1956 following suggestions that the soft top needed some time and care to erect or stow away. This attractive option had a three-piece curved rear screen and larger, more curved front windscreen, with engineering modifications made to the body shell to adopt this. The doors were completely redesigned to accept wind-down windows, and swivelling style quarterlights were fitted. A very neat set of exterior door handles was also fitted; no more bending in to pull the wire, as these models were fully lockable. The seats were also a different design and stowage bins were now provided in the footwells. Overall 6000 coupés were sold with a price hike of around £80 or so, and they weighed in at around 32lb heavier.

With 120mph top speed, the larger, much more expensive – £1357 for hardtop coupé – 1589cc Twin Cam was in production from 1958 to April 1960. Not too shy of £400 extra over an open base model with fabric roof, it had double overhead camshafts and 108hp on tap. The cylinder head was an aluminium version of the B-series engine's. Performance was vastly improved with a sub 10 second 0-60mph time. Disc brakes were sensibly fitted all round and 2111 were manufactured, with just 143 in right-hand drive, and 323 in coupé form. A chrome Twin Cam badge was fitted on the boot-lid and two more fitted upfront aside the bonnet vents.

Above and below: MGA 1600 advertising.

There were no chrome hub caps fitted. The dashboard was vinyl covered on the Twin Cam and instrumentation slightly revised.

Some engines were subject to warranty claims due to detonation and burnt oil issues, and sales quickly suffered. A low compression engine was produced that largely solved the problems, but not before the most expensive MGA's reputation had been tarnished. Both *Autocar* and *Motor* UK rival weekly magazines tested a Twin Cam, but the former magazine's acceleration performance was a lot worse than expected (0-60mph 13.3 seconds compared to *Motor*'s 9.1 seconds). Both magazines achieved around 114mph top speed, however.

"Poetry in Motion! There's nothing quite like the way its swift new horses level the hills and the way it steps through tight bends with cat-like precision." The US copyrighters were keen on portraying the extra power of the base model 1600 in 1959 with the introduction of the popular £940/£1027 (roadster/coupé) 1600, a 1588cc 80hp engine. These models were fitted with front disc brakes and still with rear drums, although there was a deluxe model with the Twin Cam's disc brake chassis.

The introduction of the 1600 also saw

1961 1600 on the seafront! Below: The updated rear lights, and the splendid 1961 specification wire wheels.

The Twin Cam dashboard (left), and unique badging (above).

Above: Interior of the Twin Cam.

The engine bay (left) and correct steel wheels (below) for the MGA Twin Cam.

A left-hand drive 1600 Mk2 dashboard.

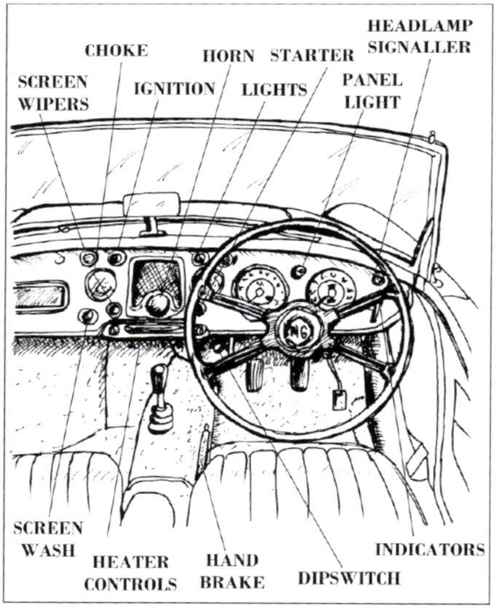

Left: MGA 1600 Mk2 dashboard layout.

internal stowage improvements behind the rear seat – enough for a weekend suitcase, with the spare wheel now mounted further back in the boot area. Rear lamps were updated, and the addition of orange indicators above were now evident. No longer were the earlier versions of the rear lamp cluster allowed to be produced on a new car due to government regulation changes.

Over 31,000 were produced in its lifetime, and the open version received a long overdue improvement to the side screens. Performance was better than the 1500 as to be expected; 100mph and 0-60mph in 14.2 seconds achieved by *Autocar* magazine in a 1590 mile 1959 test of an open car. "Typically British, this new MGA will almost certainly be as popular in foreign markets as previous models" they commented. 1959 proved to be the best sales year for the MGA with 23,000 cars delivered.

From June 1961 for a two year period, the 1600 Mk2 was sold, now with an 86bhp slightly larger 1622cc engine (achieved by increasing the bore from 75.4mm to 76.2mm). For this modest lift in cubic capacity, maximum power and torque was up by an impressive 12%. The Mk2 again was available with the deluxe trim (using up redundant Twin Cam components) and now with other detail changes. Badging and front indicator light units were also revised, and the front grille was redesigned after six years. It now took on

Recessed style grille for the last of the MGAs.

a recessed look for the vertical bars, but with the chrome surround protruding to match the surrounding bodywork.

Dashboards were now fabric covered and Rexine covering was used to aid in suppressing windscreen reflections from the scuttle in lighter coloured models. A surprising change to the rear included a raid on the Austin and Morris Mini parts bin, where the Mini's rear lamp clusters were mounted horizontally on plinths below the deck lid, thus were no longer mounted on the rear wings, allowing for a cleaner line. This change was brought about by changes in regulations in some overseas countries. Black leather cloth was now fitted to the dashboard, which helped with reflections on bright days. A final change was made to the Mk2, it was now fitted with a higher axle ratio of 4.1:1, which might have improved economy but acceleration suffered a little. Nearly 8000 Mk2s made it down the lines.

Just over 100,000 MGA cars were built in a seven-year production run and it is still a favourite model used in vintage racing. The 10,000th model was celebrated in mainstream press advertising, and this open version surfaced again in the early 2000s, still with its original gold paint and white interior. The last new car price lists shown with the MGA are for September 1962, the open version listed at £912, and the coupé at £996, these prices sandwiching the new MGB price a few weeks later.

MG MGA BODY TYPES: Two-door roadster, two-door coupé; **manufactured at:** Abingdon; **approximate number produced:** 101,181; **production span:** 1955-1962.
PERFORMANCE: (Non Twin Cam) **Top speed:** up to 100mph/160km/h; **0-60mph/100km/h:** 14.2 seconds; **average economy:** 27mpg. For faster Twin Cam, see text.
PRICE AT LAUNCH: £844 10s.
MEASUREMENTS: Length: 13ft 0in (3.96m); **width:** 4ft 10in (1.47m); **height:** 4ft 2in (1.27m); **wheelbase:** 7ft 10in (2.39m); **kerb weight:** 2030lb (922kg); **wheels:** 15in; **turning circle:** 31ft 3in (9.52m); **fuel capacity:** 10 gallons/45 litres; **boot capacity:** small – remove the spare first!
TECHNICAL: Engine types: 1489, 1589 and 1622cc. four-cyl. petrol; **gearbox:** four-speed manual; **suspension:** (front) coil springs, (rear) semi-elliptic leaf springs; **brakes:** drum all round, then Dunlop disc, see text, model dependent.
TRIM: Leather.
KEY OPTIONAL EXTRAS: HMV radio, white-wall tyres, wire wheels (with annotated removal direction indicated in the chrome), heater, windscreen washer, fog lamp, tonneau cover, radiator blind, chrome plated wheel embellishers, external luggage carrier, telescopic steering column and axle ratio of 4.55:1, de-luxe seats, competition seats, Dunlop Road-Speed tyres.

MGA media advertising slogans

1st of a new line to meet the challenge of tomorrow on road & track
The get-away car
The unsurpassed MGA
It must be an MG
Lovely, lively, luxurious
Profiled for performance
Why every MGA rates a salute! (USA)
BMC has the inside track on outdoor fun! (USA)
No wonder it holds the road! (USA)
Make yours an MG for Christmas (USA)
Poetry in motion! (USA)
The safest, fastest MG ever engineered! (USA)
Best seats in the house! (open cinema theme, USA)
Even safer! Even faster! (1600)
Pace, price, pedigree – perfect performance (1600)
Over 95mph, up to 38mpg, under £1,000
Start of a perfect day (USA)
More power to your safety (1600)
The MG has a magic of its own
One word for it – phenomenal! (Twin Cam)
More go! – More stop! (1600, USA)
They're on their way in an MGA
Designed to steal your heart!
Choose your own golden chariot (Australia)
With more power to your safety (1600 Mk2)

MG MAGNETTE FARINA SERIES

BMC was known well for badge engineering models, and the Farina-bodied Magnette launched in early 1959 was no exception. The name Magnette had been familiar to MG enthusiasts for some time, becoming well known when drivers Nuvolari and CJP Dodson won the TT in 1933 and 1934, respectively. Later on, of course, the ZA and ZB were four-door sporting saloons of the 1950s, and the Farinas were the last incarnation of this name. Essentially a very slightly beefed up Morris Oxford or Austin Cambridge (the ADO9 platform), the new Mark III Magnette (known officially as the Mark III), was held at the same retail price of £1072. The new Magnette was easily identified up front by its square chrome grille and revised bonnet moulding behind the company badge. It was more recently cruelly described as "Miss Marple meets Jane Mansfield" by the motoring press in *Classic & Sportscar* in 1989, which stated it would certainly have one in its classic car collection as it was so bad it was brilliant!

Two tone 'Duotone' paintwork was offered as an option at £18 15s which gave an eye-catching look to this executive car, dubbed by the marketeers as "a family car and a sporting car". With the earliest MG Farinas' Duotone paintwork, the boot-lid, rear side flanks up to the swage line on the rear doors and roof were the alternative colour. A different format on later Mark III cars from 1961 was adopted, whereas the alternative colour extended down to the entire length of the chrome embellishers, thus the bonnet and front door pillars were now included. The chrome strip ran the entire length down each side on all models from headlamp to rear lights. Despite a 3in shorter wheelbase, the new Mark III Magnette was 9in longer than its ZB predecessor, gaining better interior space by less wheelarch encroachment into the interior, as 14in wheels replaced the 15in units used previously.

The launch of those aforementioned Austin and Morris Farinas came a few weeks after the MG Magnette Mark III in February 1959, which in itself followed the new 'plush Farina' Wolseley and Riley models, both launched in December 1958. These were also available in

MG Magnette Mark III in Duotone.

two-tone colours, utilising yet another design scheme. The plushest of the range was the Riley 4/Sixty Eight, which strangely was the only four-cylinder Farina model fitted with a rev counter – much to the annoyance of the MG owners. The MG model was just £16 lower in price. By the end of the Farina launch period, there were no less than five models using the same basic shell and four-cylinder engines, namely: Riley 4/Sixty Eight, MG Magnette Mark III, Wolseley Fifteen Sixty, Austin Cambridge A55 and Morris Oxford V.

Into 1960 the now familiar Pininfarina body style was also adopted for use with the six-cylinder engine with Wolseley and Austin badging and uprated mechanicals. Then a plusher Vanden Plas 3-litre joined the Farina scene, eventually uprated in 1964 to a Rolls-Royce 4-litre (with built in picnic tables) in its final guise.

The MG badge was never extended to the longer six-cylinder shell, which was reserved for the Austin Westminster A99 and later A110, Wolseley 6-99 and then 6-110 and Vanden Plas 3-litre. Vanden Plas was later to replace this BMC-engined model with a Rolls-Royce B60 powered model named the Princess 4-litre R, with all the bells and whistles and a 40 per cent price hike. Below is a breakdown of how the Farina models compared on initial launch prices:

1958: Riley 4/Sixty Eight, £1028
1958: Wolseley Fifteen Sixty, £936
1959: MG Magnette Mark III, £1072
1959: Austin Cambridge A55, £802
1959: Morris Oxford V, £816
1960: Vanden Plas 3-litre, £1396
1960: Wolseley 6/99, £1254
1960: Austin A99 Westminster, £1148
1960: Vanden Plas 3-litre, £1397
1964: Vanden Plas 4-litre R, £1995

A slow (66mph and 0-60mph in 39 seconds) four-cylinder 1622cc diesel option was generally priced around £100 extra against the four-cylinder petrol cars – no doubt destined for the taxi ranks. A £70 option of automatic transmission was available on the six-cylinder cars, but neither derivative was offered for the MG Magnette, although an unpopular auto gearbox option came later.

Bold MG advertising for the Magnette Mark III in 1959.

Although there were no distinctive sports wheels – vented steel 14in units with chrome hub caps were the norm. The interior sported extra instrumentation which included an oil pressure gauge and ammeter within a distinctive MG-style binnacle featuring a speedometer in the familiar half octagonal shape with black background. Save for the binnacle, the whole fascia was wooden using Indian walnut, with wooden cappings on all four doors. A lockable vertical glovebox featured on the passenger side. Individual front buckets seats were the order of the day, whilst a wide central armrest was fitted to the rear seat. Full pile carpets (with

An early Magnette Mark III.

Rear aspect of the MG Magnette Mark III when new.

underfelt) were fitted and each vehicle occupant had access to an ashtray.

The rear end boasted a large octagonal MG badge mounted vertically on the right hand side of the boot panel, with the model name in italics flowing through it. Back in those days, 0-50mph was quoted as the de facto standard for acceleration, this twin-SU carburettor model achieving it in 13.5 seconds, some 10 seconds better than its single carburettored stablemates from Austin and Morris. The 24% performance increase was helped along by its 66hp and, I quote from the marketing blurb, "sports chosen gear ratios" and three-branch exhaust system. Across the range, automatic versions were slower. Between 1959 and mid-1961, over 15,500 Magnettes were manufactured compared to 87,000 Morris Oxford cars. Unlike the Austin and Morris derivatives, no estate version of the Magnette (or Riley or Wolseley for that matter) was ever marketed, this bodyshell was introduced in late 1960.

The earliest Farina four-cylinder cars all utilised the BMC 1489cc engine, and the second phase, confusingly referred to as the Mark IV in October 1961, although this indeed was the fourth type of four-door Magnette – had a larger 1622cc four-cylinder BMC engine. This new model came with an inch of extra wheelbase and slightly wider track, but within the same overall footprint. There were not many visual changes, although the hub caps were replaced with complete wheel covers that still included an octagonal central badge.

A 1961 model in blue, seen at an Ipswich classic car event.

Magnette Mark IV boot badging.

Rear aspect of a Magnette Mark IV.

Tall rear lamp clusters for the Magnette Mark IV.

Smart chrome wheel trim shown on a Magnette Mark IV.

A second was shaved off the 0-60mph times on the later cars, and top speed was up by around 3mph. There was now an automatic choice too. Improved anti-roll bars improved the ride and handling, noted by motoring journalists of the day.

Over 13,000 Mark IVs were produced, making a total of over 29,000 Farina style Magnettes, built away from sports car production in Abingdon, alongside other BMC products at Cowley, Oxford. The city of Oxford also used eleven models within their police force, all black with terracotta trim. Overall the Magnette may have appealed to the tweed cap and cravat brigade at the time, but the more rounded ZA and ZB 1950s predecessors seem a much more popular choice now. The last we saw of the Cowley manufactured Magnettes on the UK price lists was in March 1968, at a total price, including taxes, of £916. As a (very young) keen car spotter the author would have noted this model as a rare UK 'F' registration. The other four-door MG, the ADO16 1100 (then 1300), continued on for a further three and a half years.

Late in the season advertising for the Magnette Mark IV. By now the car had been around for six years.

MG MAGNETTE (ADO9) BODY TYPES: Four-door saloon; **manufactured at:** Cowley; **approximate number produced:** 15,676 Mark III; 13,738 Mark IV; **production span:** Mark III 1959-61; Mark IV 1961-68.
PERFORMANCE: Top speed: 85mph/137km/h; **0-60mph/100km/h:** 20 seconds; **average economy:** 25-30mpg.
PRICE AT LAUNCH: £1072 10s.
MEASUREMENTS: Length: 14ft 10in (4.52m); **width:** 5ft 3½in (1.61m); **height:** 4ft 10½in (1.49m); **wheelbase:** 8ft 4¼in (2.55m) (early 1959-61 models 8ft 3¼in); **kerb weight:** 2534lb (1150kg); **wheels:** 14in, **turning circle:** 36ft 1in (11m); **fuel capacity:** 10 gallons/45 litres; **boot capacity:** 13ft^3.
TECHNICAL: Engine types: 1489cc then 1622cc four-cylinder petrol; **gearbox:** four-speed manual, three-speed Borg Warner automatic; **suspension:** (front) independent coil springs and wishbones, (rear) live axle, leaf springs; **brakes:** drum front and drum rear, hydraulic.
TRIM: Leather/leathercloth.
KEY OPTIONAL EXTRAS: Borg Warner 35 automatic transmission on larger engine cars from 1961, Duotone colours, aluminium roof rack, seat covers, 17in badge bar, anti-mist panel, fog lamps, fire extinguisher and automatic seat front seat belt.

Magnette III and IV media advertising slogans

Completely new with a flawless pedigree
New heights of luxury in 'safety-fast' motoring!
Gear changes and changing times
What's twice as good as owning an MG?
The car that recaptures the desire to drive
The car for the young of all ages
Breeding counts (compared to K3)
The spirit and joy of a true MG
Twin carburettors for flexible power and high mpg
For pace and prestige
An automatic choice
Pedigree saloon with debonair lines
Double thrill, double value
Streets ahead in the short run, Miles ahead in the long run

ADO16 1100/1300 SERIES

Three years on from the launch of the radically new Austin Seven and Morris Mini Minor, the October 1962 Earls Court London Motor Show was the platform the British Motor Corporation used to proudly show another front-wheel drive model with transverse engine. The Morris 1100 was launched earlier in the year, and became the forerunner to the ubiquitous ADO16. The MG stand also had a new model, its MG 1100, based on the same platform as its cheaper stablemate, and available in two-door or four-door types, (£702 and £714 respectively).

Up front was the familiar large MG grille, and round chrome-surrounded indicator/side lamp units replaced oblong types used on other ADO16 models present and future. An attractive chrome strip was fitted halfway up the body sides, and this gradually swept downwards towards the rear. It formed the border for the optional Duotone paintwork, if ordered at £15 extra, the darker colour also featured on the bonnet, boot-lid and roof. To complete the look, chrome hub caps were fitted to the wheels, each with the octagonal MG badge in the centre, and large bumper overriders were soon fitted to match the rest of the plusher ADO16 range. It was quite appropriate that after some 40 years, the MG name was the first of several ADO16 models to become available on what was essentially a Morris car, with Austin, then Vanden Plas, Wolseley and Riley joining the range within a few years. Many, but not all, of the MG 1100 two-door cars produced were for export.

The transversely mounted engine upfront, a first for MG, and of course front-wheel drive, proved the model could carry up to five occupants in comfort, all within its just over 12ft length. The advertising was certainly punchy, aimed at the fast-moving young family man. A Duotone 1100 advert featured the front of a car bursting out of the magazine page: "You sly old fox you! Trust you to have your bread buttered on both sides …", going on to mention the all independent Hydrolastic suspension (a first for an MG model), and "So

Early advertising for a Duotone 1100.

American advertising, the 'Sports Sedan' MG 1100.

you've got MG pace and verve ... limousine comfort."

Over and above the (later) Austin and Morris cars, the MG models certainly had better interior appointments on offer. Restyled plusher seats, a walnut-veneer dashboard and two-tone door cards. Thicker carpeting was fitted in a variety of colours: Rose Taupe, Almond Green or Blue. Road testers found the new model favourable, commenting on easy access to both front and rear over the low sills. However, on not such a good note, *Autocar* magazine commented in a late 1962 road test, "Just below 70mph there was a very unpleasant booming in the body ..." and "somewhere on the engine bulkhead a persistent rattle annoyed us." It also commented that top speed was some 7mph faster than the Morris at 85mph and overall, despite the improved performance available, there was no significant extra fuel burnt through the twin SU HS2 type semi-downdraught carburettors. The Mk1 was indeed popular; over 116,000 units were manufactured.

Niggly comments were made by owners at the time concerning interior controls in the main. These included wiper and washer controls at opposite ends of the fascia, if a key fob was used it would completely cover

MG 1100 engine bay, illustration when new.

Rear aspect shown in early advertising.

MG 1300 early dashboard with strip speedometer.

up the ignition warning light, not helpful if a fan belt snaps. On two-door models it was almost impossible to keep the vertically hinged rear side windows open using the over-centre catches, they would simply close due to the fitment of their draft sealing strip. The heater was awkward to work: the water valve control gave little adjustment between 'cook' and 'freeze'. In any case, it was near on impossible to reach the heater quadrant controls when belted in with the optional static seat belts, and the only way round this was to juggle them, in transit, with an available foot. Safety Fast!

A last minute entry to the range before the Mk2s came onboard was the MG 1300. The 1275cc engine borrowed from the Mini Cooper S, Austin-Healey Sprite and MG Midget was also being offered to all of the more opulent ADO16s, namely Vanden Plas, Wolseley and Riley. However this was no rival to the faster and lighter Mini Cooper S, as Charles Griffin (BMC chief engineer) pointed out at a press conference to the media in summer 1967, the MG now had a single carburettor 1300 achieving 0-60mph in a leisurely 17 seconds.

The Mk2 model, available from October 1967, and in line with other ADO16 models, had a comprehensively restyled interior and now at last we saw an MG saloon with a rev counter (the Magnette never had one). There were three large round dashboard dials that replaced the basic and very non-MG looking strip style display of the earlier cars. A far more attractive three-spoke sporting steering wheel replaced the rather ordinary unit used in the Mk1. Seats were still thicker and better trimmed over and above the cheaper models, but were updated too. The wood veneer was of far higher quality than that used in the rather plasticky and yellow finished earlier Mk1 cars, the dash top was of thicker moulding, the door cards were refreshed, but the handy front quarterlight windows remained.

All these improvements brought improved sound deadening, something that was criticised in the Mk1 cars. Under the bonnet there were now twin SU semi-downdraught carburettors and a high output dynamo, "The muscles of the Mk2 MG 1300 – they will punch you up to 40 in 6 short seconds," claimed the BMC press office. Having the

Speed effect on an MG 1100 press advert. "You sly old fox, you!"

optional automatic AP in-the-sump gearbox fitted to the MG 1300 Mk2 created no slouch either, with late 1968 road test cars achieving 93mph and a creditable 0-60mph in around 13 seconds. Fuel consumption took a very slight blow, with an overall figure of 25.4mpg achieved by *Autocar* magazine published in its 21st December 1968 issue. Worthy of note is that this excellent automatic gearbox, which made its debut in 1965, was four-speed, with a free-wheel facility in first gear, not recommended for tough hill descents!

A keen in-house last minute rival that should not go without mention, was the Austin 1300GT from 1969, always in four-door format, and arguably, more sportier looking than the MG in a bunch of vivid and daring colours, complete with black spoked wheel trims. Aimed at the extrovert popular 'GT' market, the more modern approach was to fit a vinyl roof and all black interior with standard reclining front seats, which the MG never saw. The GT received much more contemporary advertising at a time when the MG 1300 saw none at all, and thus the GT's sales were higher. The engine and its ancillaries, were almost identical.

The last road test published on the MG 1300 was by *Motor* magazine in early 1969 on a manual version, just ahead of the aforementioned 1300GT launch. "At last, real performance," read the title of the report. OOH 740G was thrashed to 95mph, and more was available if the wind had allowed. Two doors, twin carburettors and a revised final ratio gave this car a 0-60mph acceleration time of 13.1 seconds

The last of the Mk2 MG 1300s (two-door versions) were advertised in the new car tables in January 1972 at £993, following a nine year production run and slightly outlasting first the Morris and then the Austin 1100 and 1300s by a few months. 26,240 were produced overall for both home and export market, particularly the USA.

A 1967 MG 1100 in immaculate condition.

MG 1100 Mk2 when new.

MG 1300 Mk2 when new.

MG 1100/1300 BODY TYPES: Two-door saloon, four-door saloon; **manufactured at:** Cowley; **approximate number produced:** 116,827 (1100) and 26,240 (1300); **production span:** 1962-71.
PERFORMANCE: (1100) **Top speed:** 85mph/135km/h; **0-60mph/100km/h:** 17 sec; **average economy:** 30mpg.
PRICE AT LAUNCH: £702 (Two-door), £714 (four-door).

The Mk2 dashboard (1300 shown).

MEASUREMENTS: **Length:** 12ft 2¾in (3.73m); **width:** 5ft ½in (1.54m); **height:** 4ft 4½in (1.33m); **wheelbase:** 7ft 9½in (2.37m); **kerb weight:** 1848lb (838kg); **wheels:** 12in; **turning circle:** 35ft 7in (10.85m); **fuel capacity:** 8 gallons/36 litres; **boot capacity:** 9½ft³.

TECHNICAL: **Engine types:** 1098cc and 1275cc four-cylinder petrol; **gearbox:** four-speed manual; **suspension:** (front) wishbones with Hydrolastic and damper units; (rear) trailing arms with damper units, Hydrolastic interconnected with the front; **brakes:** disc front and drum rear.

TRIM: Ambla, optional leather.

KEY OPTIONAL EXTRAS: Duotone paint, laminated glass screen, leather upholstery (£12), white sidewall or Weathermaster tyres, roof rack, reversing light, driving lights, front and rear seat belts (until standardised in front), automatic transmission on 1100/1300 models, radio, reclining front seats, heated rear window, exhaust trim and badge bar.

MG 1100 and 1300 media advertising slogans

We've marketed the corner
Soft top – hard ride, hard top – soft ride (18/80 v 1100)
The most advanced MG of all time
Smile when you say small … (USA)
Anything to declare? (USA)
Family room … Engine room … (USA)
Who needs rear wheels? (USA)
Please don't drink the suspension system … (USA)
You sly old fox, you!
Fresh summer wind
The muscles of the Mark II MG 1300

The unusual MG Princess sold in the USA. Just 154 were made.

MGB AND MGC SERIES

As production of the seven-year-old MGA drew to a close, the new MGB was being prepared for display to the public for the first time at the London Motor Show in October 1962. The press had revealed diagrams, photos and comprehensive articles in late September, informing readers of a new body with bigger engine for the MGA's slightly smaller chassis-less successor. In the flesh, it afforded quite a few favourable comments from members of the public, who were also discovering another British first, the brand new Ford Cortina Mk1, at the same show.

Alongside the existing Midget on the show stand, and with more rewarding lines and a slightly bigger footprint allowing for more interior room and boot space than its stable-mate, here was another brand new roadster model. It was smart, modern, had two doors with wind-up windows and a non-detachable fabric roof.

With the B there was no association with any other company, as there had been with the Austin-Healey-based Midget. It was true that, at first glance, the MGB looked similar to the MG Midget/Austin Healey Sprite II, now on their second excursion to the London Earls Court show, but the MGB had all new panels, and a new 1798cc four-cylinder engine fitted in a monocoque shell of unitary construction. The new B-series engine was a vast improvement on the previous B-series unit of 1622cc used in the later MGAs, with more benefit to maximum torque than to power at the top end.

Top: An immaculate early roadster, with the rear lamp cluster shown below.

The original colour range was Chelsea Grey, Iris Blue, Black, Tartan Red and Old English White, with British Racing Green following about three months later. A special cutaway MGB was displayed at various Motor Shows. This forerunner to the lengthways sliced-in-two MGB GT that followed three years later was different. It was mounted on a circular display and featured all of its chassis in one piece, with the bodywork removed rear of the windscreen, leaving just the seating and some of the floor.

An early left-hand drive MGB roadster.

The cutaway vehicle that was shown at the various Motor Shows.

An early roadster.

The road testers were impressed, *Autocar* having tested it for its 26th October 1962 Motor Show issue. The test car, an early production model 523CBL, achieved a top speed of 105mph with extra power over the smaller Midget, and a 0-60mph acceleration time of around 12.2 seconds, some eight seconds faster than its small stablemate. Average economy on this heavier model was 21.4mpg overall (the whole test), compared to a much more refreshing 33mpg with the Midget.

The 1964 Brussels Autosalon Show had a stand featuring the MG Coune Berlinette, a very stylish coach-built example, with definite Italian overtones. By the 1960s Coune had started reworking a few cars, particularly making attractive estate versions of the Mercedes 220SE and BMW 700. Featuring a taller windscreen, altered headlamps, a hard top roof, decent rear glass treatment, curved boot lid and round rear lamps, it had more changes made to the standard version than could be listed here. Up front though, was the familiar front apron, bumper and grille.

The prototype was hand-made with lots of welding and metal changes, whilst the 56 or so production models made use of fibreglass. The Brussels car ended up with BMC and a licence was discussed, but in the end MG decided on its own version.

For some time before this, the B had seen a number of outside manufacturers offering an alternative roof to Abingdon's optional hardtop for the car, it was particularly unpleasant to drive in winter in cold conditions – the long cold winter of 1963 springs to mind – as the cloth roof did little to keep in any heat. In blizzard conditions, it was entirely possible to have to put up with the ingress of snow, even with the canvas hood held firmly in position. Some of these hardtop conversions can be seen fitted to early rally cars where often snowy mountain passes would be endured. One manufacturer was John Aylstone & Co, London, which provided a very tidy looking hardtop made in fine grain glass-fibre for £48, incorporating a panoramic rear window, rear quarterlights and aluminium rain gutters. A sky-view roof window was also available for an extra £10. Other versions were the Bermuda hardtop, with five glazed areas, that was also supplied for the Midget/Sprite and Triumph Spitfire. The Williams & Pritchard hardtop was priced at £47 (ex-works) and had tailored headlining included. The later Ashley Line from Bishop's Stortford, which sold the world's largest range of hardtops for sports cars, and its stylish MGB roadster conversion incorporated a new boot lid and massive rear panoramic window to the design. This sold for around £100.

GT launched

So, complementing the roadster from 1965, came the new fastback MGB GT. Weighing in at around 160lb heavier than the roadster, the new model looked distinctly different from the rear, with a big curved wide glass and metal tailgate, with concealed hinges and large windows on each side. Up front, the windscreen was taller than the roadster.

1966 advertising for the new fastback GT.

An early press car reveals its capacious boot.

It was styled by Syd Enever's department at Abingdon, and the final touches were by Pininfarina who was a consultant to British Motor Corporation at the time. 21,835 Mk1 GT models were produced, followed by 91,207 Mk2 versions to 1971, but the roadster still outsold the GT by a factor of over 2:1.

It must be said that the GT is strictly a 2+2 as rear seat accommodation was decidedly a challenge for any occupants over ten years of age. The short vertical section of the new rear seat could be folded down for longer loads, and an extra 8in of load length was gained.

The GT model was launched at the October 1965 London Motor Show for £998 8s 9d. Accompanying a red GT with black leather seats, another full-size car was cut lengthwise and placed on a rotating stand to reveal a real

The GT had these attractive motifs behind the opening side windows.

3D cutaway car, and the extra soundproofing, anti-roll bar at the front and stiffer springs were also evident. It was a great way to see how all the engine and gearbox components would work, as it was literally sliced down the middle, with just the pistons left uncut one side, and showing the combustion chambers on the opposing side. The cutaway model was later revised into Mk2 specification and shown again at the Turin Motor Show in 1967. It has now been preserved and can be seen on display at the British Motor Museum at Gaydon, and is often affectionately referred to as the 'divorce car'.

It was not long before the boys in blue's heads were turned, as the GT would make an ideal compact and fast vehicle for their fleets, and East Sussex constabulary ordered four such vehicles without rear seats for use as patrol cars.

Heavier MGC launched

After two years of MGB production, plans were afoot to produce a six-cylinder car as a top of the range model to replace the Austin-Healey 3000, also produced at Abingdon. Syd Enever's team at Abingdon looked at possible engine power, including the Australian built 'Light Six', a 2433cc Freeway engine that was basically the 1622cc B-series with two extra cylinders. Several prototypes were built (some of which were sold off in the early 1970s) with various wheel and tyre combinations, but as the Australian engine was not to be built in the UK, they looked nearer home and found the Longbridge Austin 3-litre power plant would indeed fit, albeit there had to be a change to the bonnet, a higher compression ratio and the radiator had to be moved forwards by about 8in. The front floor pan was also different, changes had to be made to accommodate the extra parts and wider automatic gearbox, plus further changes were made to the front suspension set up. As a note of interest, the Austin 3-litre was built as a rear-wheel drive car, on a body originally designed for a front-wheel drive configuration. In all, despite some unfavourable comments from the press about the lack of sparkle that the seven-bearing 2912cc engine had – and the car's understeer when cornering under pressure – it sold a little slower than the MGB with production ending in 1969.

In late 1967 the new car was displayed at the London Motor show alongside the GT, thus the more powerful – and 345lb heavier MGC had joined the line-up. "High performance grand touring luxury, quickest way of taking to the hills without robbing a bank ..." stated the advert copy writers. It cost an extra £253 more than the B, and was available in both roadster and GT bodies that sold in more or less equal numbers. To the casual eye the C looked the same as the B save for the badging, slightly taller wheels/tyres and a distinct wide hump on the

1967 MGC advertising, the production run was short.

Left: An immaculate MGC GT accelerating away from Helmingham Hall classic car show, 2024. Right: Rear aspect of the MGC GT.

aluminium bonnet with a curved over chrome strip towards its leading edge. This covered the extra size of the front carburettor on the nearside feeding its straight six engine. Oh, and it had tiltable seats, a leather covered steering wheel and two-speed wipers! The overhead valve power unit was borrowed from the only BMC Landcrab, the Austin 3-litre, and this car was launched that same very week. Top speed of the C averaged around 123mph as tested by the motoring press, with a 0-60mph acceleration time of around 10 seconds. Downton Engineering also produced a few tuned examples too with changes to the manifold and cylinder head, and works cars raced at Sebring, Florida. More than

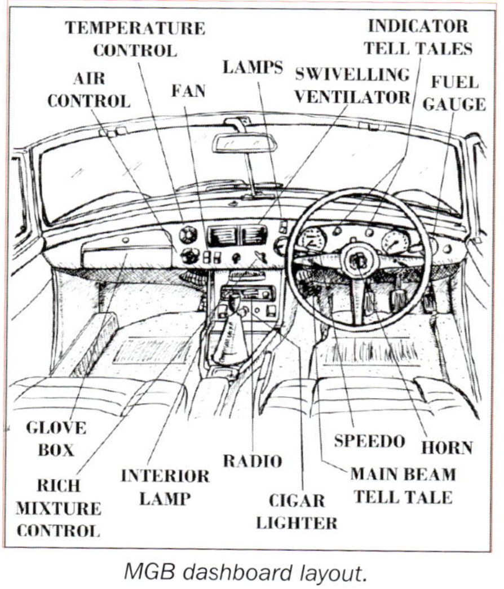

MGB dashboard layout.

10,000 Austin 3-litres were produced over a five-year production run, compared to 4552 MGC roadsters and 4457 MGC GTs. University Motors took the last 150 MGCs and upgraded these final models, offering some with Downton tuning kits.

MGB Mk2

Enter the Mk2, as also in 1967 the MGB model range was generally updated, although Mk2 badges were never fitted. An all synchromesh gearbox was now utilised, and the 18GD engine was fitted. For more reliable electrics, a modern alternator replaced the ageing dynamo. The three-speed Borg Warner 35 automatic transmission now on offer was an option unlikely to have been requested by the police force, who were seen in the odd B here and there. Only around 4000 MGBs built had this option fitted and it was deleted mid-1970s. USA cars had a rather ugly padded facia to comply with local crash protection regulations for the 1968 season.

Well before the Special Tuning department of British Leyland breathed on the performance side of the MGB, Special Motor Repairs of North London was on the scene in 1968 with its extrovert MGB. The SMR conversion was a top end job only to keep labour costs down, having reworked the head to achieve 10:1 compression ratio and fitted a choked down 45DCOE carburettor. Although the fuel consumption graph was practically a flat line, with the most economic speed being 60mph, the best top speed obtained under test in a 1968 *Motor* specialist conversions article, was 115mph in one direction, with a

0-60mph of 10.4 seconds, over two seconds quicker than the standard car. Minilite wheels completed the picture. A roadster, NJJ 183E, was the subject car, but this seems to have vanished from the DVLA website.

Late season 1969 changes included the adoption of a new matt black recessed grille (to match the new Midget style), with a thick chrome surround and rectangular chrome inlay. Despite the MG motif being moved down, the raised bonnet pressing that reflected where the badge sat in front was not modified. This certainly looked a little odd in the same way as the two-door Range Rover castellations for the original bonnet mirrors were not deleted when door mirrors became standard. Smart wide-rim black and silver Rostyle wheels were now fitted, but most export cars had the wire wheels. The cockpit remained largely unaltered, except that reclining seats were made standard, and cheaper ambla trim replaced the leather versions. The emblems were changed including a GT motif and a British Leyland badge appeared on the front wings. The MG MGB GT retailed at £1268.

USA advertising, early 1970s.

In the very early 1970s, in true Carnaby Street style, both the Midget and MGB roadster were subject to some rather suggestive magazine advertising (not included in this book). This type of advert wouldn't be allowed today, for obvious reasons, although they could have been a lot worse. The adverts, some featuring scantily clad young ladies, were run by the leading weekly magazines, with the worst of them only being published in monthly *Car* magazine as far as the author knows. The tag line on each was "Your Mother Wouldn't Like It" with the inference being that a mother would not be pleased to see her son in the company of the subject, but the young gent would have loved it! Given that the readership of the magazines was mainly male, the author can only assume the image of the cars was uplifted and the advertising agencies did their job well.

Triplex also got in on the act and published an advert for its heated rear window option, displaying three images of a steamed up GT with the caption "A reminder to young lovers everywhere." More subdued images used for later rubber-bumper cars advertising included the script "Some day, you'll settle down with a nice sensible girl, nice sensible house and a nice sensible family saloon," and "You can do it in an MG." Even the American advertising agents were up to these tricks, although weren't quite so revealing. One advert read "The new MGB/GT can help save your marriage" and went on to suggest that the car understood a man, knew how to flatter the better half, had room for the children, would be comfortable at the most dressed up affairs, and was designed for a family budget.

The 1971 model year cars had improvements to the hood mechanism and an uprated heater, and in May, the 250,000th MGB was produced, with, at that point, a fifth of a million exported. There were also now automatic boot and bonnet opening stays. In late 1971, the more up to date (and lighter) Morris Marina was launched with two engine options, the larger of which was the 1798cc MGB unit. Both cars generate a distinctive hollow exhaust sound, and back in the mid-1970s it was entirely possible to hear what you thought was an MG approaching only to be confronted with a new 1800cc Morris! The Marina 1.8TC was available as saloon, estate and coupé, but the model was replaced by the O series 1700 in the late 1970s, as the MGB continued on. Further changes for the 1972 model year included a revised facia with rocker switches and face level fresh air vents plus other cosmetic changes.

British Leyland Special Tuning, of Abingdon, developed a super Stage 3 tuning kit for the B at £160 plus fitting and testing. The conversion added around 6mph to the top speed and shaved more than a second and a half off the 0-60mph acceleration time. Contemporary road testers loved the compatibility of all the parts, remarking that the kit was as good as it could get. The whole kit consisted of:

- *1½in SU carburettors £26.73*
- *Installation kit £14.50*
- *Polished cylinder head £55.75*
- *Competition head gasket £0.90*
- *Revised camshaft £17*
- *Champion N64Y plugs £0.80.*

In a 1972 *Motor* magazine test, a young staff tester named Tony Dron (who later went on to manage *Classic Cars* magazine) said: "The Stage 3 B is a great long distance cruiser which we thoroughly recommend to those with the bread for the extra gas, as they say." Also in 1972, Abingdon built an orange SSV1 safety car based on the GT body. It demonstrated all the potential safety features that Abingdon may need to add over the following years. Some were an insight, some plain absurd, including a large roof-mounted periscope aimed at the potential US market. There were airbags, special bumpers, and additional strength bars built in. This car is now housed at the British Motor Museum at Gaydon.

By the 1973 model year, there was a new style steering wheel, padded arm pull/armrests on the doors and cloth seats were phased in at this point (the roadsters retained the ambla trim for obvious reasons). Also new was the change to a black plastic front grille with chrome surround that now sported a vertical

One of the last chrome bumper GT models poses at Aldeburgh, Suffolk.

The last of the chrome bumper UK MGBs had this rubber trim on the bumper caps.

centre bar. The less-favoured automatic option was discontinued in mid-1973, and windscreen wipers were now black finished.

V8 introduction

August 1973 saw the introduction of the mighty MGB GT V8, which has become one of the most respected MGs of all time. Vehicles featured on all the main UK magazine covers only: it was not to be sold for overseas markets, as the 3.5-litre engine was also in short supply. Leslie Lambourne, MG chief, was interviewed by *Motor* magazine upon its launch. "The fear is, if only a small quantity is shipped to the United States, then the result could be many cancelled orders for the B by potential owners hoping to obtain one of the scarce V8s. The upshot would be a fall in total MG sales."

Tuner Ken Costello had been offering a very tidy V8 conversion on both roadster and GT platforms for a relatively short while until now, identified by a different bonnet with large bulge at the rear, and its own distinctive front grille and badging. However, British Leyland stopped the supply of new V8s to Costello at the same time, as they were in short supply, and needed in P6 Rovers and Range Rovers, and it still had a firm contract to supply Morgan. The Costello conversion had been offered for £2522 (GT), and one or two early examples were brought back to Costello for warranty repairs to the gearbox, as the unchanged unit really was at its limits to cope with the extra power on board when pushed. The box was subsequently changed.

The factory version, the MG MGB GT V8, had its own distinctive alloy road wheels, overdrive was standard, and police

A 1972 GT with V8 conversion.

V8 badging with the newer style grille.

V8 style wheel.

specification suspension was used. The large ex-Buick V8 and its cooling system were somehow shoe-horned ahead of the

Late model roadster at Helmingham Hall.

GTs bulkhead. The engine was an all alloy construction, originally from the USA which is well documented elsewhere and conveniently there was no discernible difference in weight, but its performance was more than impressive, not to mention that lovely exhaust note! There was a closer set of gear ratios on the V8 cars, and like the Costello cars mentioned above, the final drive ratio was placed at 3.07:1.

Motoring Which? consumer magazine was well known for its very frank opinions on new cars. It road-tested an early production V8 and commented that it came with 30 delivery defects. Whilst the car proved reliable, it turned up at its offices with 18 paint defects (chips, scratches runs, a bad finish and dents), the front wheels were out of alignment, the gearbox was overfilled with oil, there was damage to the prop shaft shield and battery carrier, both doors were leaking and there was a misaligned driver's door. Two small children obviously posed looking very uncomfortable while attempting to sit upright in the back, with the comment "Clearly not ideal for family transport." In conclusion, *Motoring Which?* (it would always blank over the number plate for its tests) commented in its 1974 road test of the V8 "The MGB GT V8 was great fun to drive, splendid as a sports car. But its high wind noise, harsh ride and heavy steering detracted a great deal from it as a long distance tourer." Top speed seen by this journal was 124mph and a 0-60mph acceleration of 8.4 seconds with an overall consumption of 22mpg. The magazine even employed a 'thief' who found that the car was very easy to break into, but he could not defeat the column lock for some time.

The BGT V8 went on and was produced along with the revised October 1974 rubber bumper cars, and bowed out after three years, last listed at £3881 on the price lists in October 1976. As the V8 was never officially exported, it was a shame that it did not get to retain those chrome bumpers until it ended production. 2591 were produced, all in fastback GT format, although plenty of enthusiasts, and firms, have converted open roadsters to run with this 3.5-litre V8 engine since, and of course we saw the 1992 launch of the RV8 two decades later. One such specialist company was Lenham in Kent. Its attractive roadster kept the higher GT windscreen – better for taller drivers – and it had a distinctive shorter boot lid.

After one year of sales in the USA, the First Anniversary MGB GT Special was announced. 1000 such models were available for the entire USA market and included some extra refinements to celebrate: a plaque, 16in wood steering wheel and a vibrationless non-glare racing type wing mirror. The existing large electric tachometer, 60-spoke wire wheels, twin SU carburettors for better acceleration and other key items were added to the contemporary adverts for good measure. During the mid-1970s and before the chrome bumper models ended, new MGBs exported to the USA were fitted with triple windscreen wipers of smaller length to get round regulations, this idea was never adopted in the UK.

Rubber bumper and later cars

In autumn 1974 the entire look of the MGB and Midget ranges radically changed in production with the introduction of the (then) controversial rubber bumpers. Changes were made to sheet metal to accept these front and rear, plus raised suspension by an inch and a half and

A rubber bumper roadster.

consequent ride height to allow the bumpers to sit at the right 'federal' height. This was from chassis number 360301. Again, in the USA, to get round federal laws, the last of the chrome bumper cars had enormous crash can overriders fitted at the front from the previous September, and they did nothing for the cars looks. The fastback GT version was at this point deleted from the American order books.

In August 1975 it was announced there would be 750 commemorative Jubilee GTs built for the UK market to mark half a century of motoring heritage, although strictly speaking the first MG produced was in 1924. These models had thick gold striping (the chrome side rails underneath were now painted body colour), gold cast alloy wheels and were all GTs not roadsters. The British Racing Green looked fantastic, and the quota included the V8. Tinted glass and overdrive came as standard, as did black carpets and headrests on the black cloth seats. A larger three-spoke steering wheel helped with low speed parking using the heavier wheels. Most, but not all, of the cars had a brass plate on the glovebox quoting its number. A Golden Anniversary MGB was also offered in the USA in 1975 again following the 50 years of MG production in the UK.

In June 1975 the overdrive option for all models was made standard, as was the adoption of the V8 instrumentation. Later on the MGB Special was marketed for the USA market. The car included four extra features to be made standard equipment including an AM/FM radio, boot mounted luggage rack, chrome wheel trim rings, MGB striping and graphics on the lower body, all for $5150. The subject car shown was black.

In August 1976, for the 1977 model year, specification changes included: a redesigned instrument panel once again, including an electric clock and switches that illuminated at night, seat belt and handbrake warning lamps added, an improvement to the steering rack gearing to reduce turning effort, single flick windscreen washers, a smaller steering wheel, head restraints were fitted, seat upholstery was now supplied as striped cloth, the overdrive switch was added to the top of the gear lever, the adoption of halogen headlamp

Indicator unit in a rubber bumper MGB.

Front rubber bumper of the MGB.

Late MGB series USA advertising.

Cloth seats for the GT.

bulbs, the addition of anti-roll bars front and rear for increased handling stability. The roadster gained a zip-down rear window for better ventilation with the top still up, and there was a new system of heating controls that were easier to use.

The Queen's Silver Jubilee was celebrated that spring and a Pageant Blue Silver Jubilee GT was built and used as a raffle prize, being displayed ahead of the raffle at a local dealer in Abingdon. The story was that special permission had to be gained from Buckingham Palace to fit unique graphics on the front wings and bonnet. Silver striping was added down the body flanks and the car, GBW 500S, had a number of enthusiastic owners who kept the road mileage to an absolute minimum. It survives to this day.

After this point there were not too many production changes, but final 1970s cars delivered to the USA were single carburettor only and had just 65bhp, with power lacking so much it could have been outpaced by an elderly MGA.

The LE models.

In the final stages of production, Abingdon announced two limited edition models, the LE cars, with full page advertising in the press. There were to be 420 roadsters finished in Bronze Metallic paintwork with orange and brown trim, and 580 GT models in Pewter Metallic

Late GT UK advertising.

Paint with silver grey trim. Both variants had unique graphics featuring a British flag, striped fabric seating, limited edition badges, a black front spoiler and a passenger door mirror as standard. The announcement also mentioned that 208 of the roadster models (referred to as the tourer) would have painted wire wheels, whilst the remaining 212 would have alloys. Retail prices for these run out models were £6108 for the roadster and £6576 for the fastback GT. Two were destined for British Motor Heritage, the bronze roadster is referred to below and safely resides in Abingdon Museum. The last MGB built was in August of 1980, but dealer stocks remained until late 1981, with even the LE models proving as hard to sell, despite advertising. During its 18-year life the MGB had no really strong rival, except for its TR cousins from Triumph. A later contender would have been the Datsun 240 and 260Z coupés, although the reputation of these was tarnished due to corrosion issues and resultant depreciation.

There was a huge public outcry that the UK car industry could lose the MG name when news of the closure of production leaked out. *Motor* magazine held a readers' competition for designs for a new MG two-seater that should be based on current or future BL components, two or three months before the last very cars were rolling off the production line. The magazine received 490 high quality entries, and felt it to be a massive response. The 30 year old winner, G D Thomson, actually worked at the styling department of Talbot. His winning entry, whilst angular and sharp, with a steeply raked windscreen, vaguely looked like a mid-1980s Scimitar SS1, but interestingly adopted the two-tone dark-at-the-bottom approach like the forthcoming MG Metro Turbo. During the time staff were digesting the information that the Abingdon

Webasto folding sunroofs on GTs were a popular option in the 1970s.

This experimental SSV1 GT safety car now resides at the Gaydon Heritage museum, UK. Yes, that is a periscope on the roof ...

Below: The last roadster now resides at the Abingdon museum.

factory was set to close in 1980, Aston Martin's then chairman formed a consortium to save the ailing MG plant. William Towns was commissioned to produce a face-lifted MGB for production into 1981. The consortium collapsed as not enough Japanese investors could be found. The proposed Aston-MG concept largely kept the MGB's lines but used a higher windscreen and doors, and the old chrome grille surround was incorporated in the plastic front bumper. Again, a darker bottom section of the body and revised rear lighting allowed for an overall lower look. When the photos were released in April of 1981, an Aston Martin spokesman stated "A lot of people still believe it was all a publicity stunt, but there was a real determination by the company to make it work".

In 1988, six years after the MG name was resurrected by the introduction of the Metro, it was discovered that out of the 750 pressing tools that were used to make the MGB bodywork, most were still available and in storage. The market for rebodying early MGs was certainly a strong proposition, as some spares were starting to dry up and the cars

Interior of the last roadster with striped trim.

vital lifting inches at the last minute. It was successfully placed into position using a specially made rotating jig that was fixed to the body using the bumper mounting points. After a couple of hours including a near miss with an expensive chandelier inside the building, it was reassembled and

were popular with many still on the road. A Heritage scheme was introduced at Faringdon, near Oxford and complete new donor shells became available, thus extending the longevity of this classic model. A couple of years later, the first completed conversion using such a shell was shown to Rover management along with a fuel injected V8, and upon seeing these, the decision was soon made to commence the RV8 project.

Back in the summer of 2011, HOK 681W – one of the last MGB roadsters made and in final LE specification – was in need of a new display home, away from BMHT Museum at Gaydon. What better than the local Abingdon authority-run museum in the old Grade 1 listed timber-framed courtrooms in its birth town Abingdon, some 45 miles to the south? It would be the star attraction once the museum refurbishment was completed in 2012, not to mention its biggest item on display. But getting it into the old building seemed impossible.

After much planning with removal experts, late in 2011 the Bronze Metallic roadster was prepared for a vertical Liftlux scissor-lift ride through the narrow but tall 17th century windows on the first floor, some 30ft above pavement level. The heavy components were removed; wheels, both axles, engine, gearbox, bonnet, bumpers and front windshield – vital if the car was to get through with just over an inch clearance (30mm) from the open museum windows. It caused quite a local spectacle, with the lorry crane giving extra

now looks a million dollars in the refurbished museum which reopened to the public in 2012. At least it is safe in the knowledge that it cannot be stolen! It is not until you visit the museum that you realise just how tight the clearance was for the MGB body to be inserted through the central window of the aperture.

To my great personal surprise, and being a keen genealogist, it is parked next to an exhibit that details the history of my great (times seven) grandfather, one John Alder, an Abingdon cooper in the 1700s, who won the local lottery and passed his vast winnings over to the people of the town and also bought race horses and a stage coach. Did my then lucky descendants eventually work at the factory here 150 years later? I note that one of many MG suppliers names was indeed Alford & Alder …

MGB AND MGC BODY TYPES: two-door roadster, two-door hatchback coupe GT (from 1965); **manufactured at:** Abingdon; **approximate number produced:** 523,836. Note 9000 Roadsters produced from CKD in Enfield then Zetland, Australia (1963-1972); **Production span:** 1962-1980. New British Heritage shells available from 1988.
PERFORMANCE: Four-cylinder cars: top speed: 104mph/170km/h; 0-60mph/100km/h: 12.5 sec; average economy: 28mpg. V8 cars: top speed: 125mph/200km/h; 0-60mph/100km/h: 8.5 sec; average economy: 23mpg. MGC: top speed:

MGB media advertising slogans

Superlative M.G.B. with 1800cc engine (original advert)
Look, they've got an MG
Just in time for the summer, open roads, sunshine, lots of fun ...
Winning ways – all through the range (Le Mans reference)
Proved on the track, right on the road
Success after success, that's BMC engineering!
BMC wins in the tough one! (Targa Florio event)
Behold the fast, bold and blatantly beautiful ...
When you get a sudden irresistible urge to go nowhere in particular ...
MGC most powerful MG ever
Much more than meets the eye! (MGC)
Nuova 3 Litri MGC. Secura E Veloce Bella Vettura Inglese
Your mother wouldn't like it (several types)
The great escape car. MGB GT (USA)
The new MGB/GT can help save your marriage. Read why (USA)
The Genuine Grand Touring car (USA)
It says more about you than you'd ever say about yourself (USA)
People don't buy the MGB because they are different, but because they are (USA)
First on the scene. And still one jump ahead (USA)
For those who want to get involved instead of just getting around (USA)
Trim, taut and pure (USA)
Think of it as a well co-ordinated athlete (USA)
MGB presents the world's biggest sunroof (USA)
The Golden Anniversary MGB (USA)
Still built with a marvellous device called the human hand (USA)
It's the real GT they're after
The sports car for the enthusiast
Sport the real thing (several types)
You can do it in an MG (several types)
If you've just bought a Reliant Scimitar GTE, a Datsun 240Z or an Alfa Romeo 2000 GTV, this will ruin your day (V8)
Some day, you'll settle down with a nice sensible girl, a nice sensible house and a nice sensible family saloon. Some day
Octagon spirit is a wild ride at Le Mans
If it weren't for the 12th improvement, you could see the other 11
MGB. The wide-open sports car (USA)
There is a reason why more Americans buy MGB than any other convertible. Here it is (USA)
Sun, wind, action. MGB (USA)
Widen your horizons (USA)
The classic breed (USA roadster)
Ladies (young) are not expected to
It lacks many of the things you'd expect to find in a sports car
The MGB Limited Edition
MGB Limited Edition. Unlimited fun (USA)
Psychologists say a saloon car is a wife and a sports car is a mistress (1979 GT)
Why a brand new MGB is already a valuable collector's item

120mph/190km/h; 0-60mph/100km/h: 10 sec; average economy: 18mpg.
PRICE AT LAUNCH: £949 15s 3d (1962, MGB), £1101 16s 8d (MGC roadster).
MEASUREMENTS: Length: 12ft 9¼in (3.83m), rubber bumpers cars 13ft 2¼in (3.95m) note: add 1½in for GT model); **width:** 5ft 0in (1.5m); **height:** 4ft 1½in (1.23m) but rubber bumper models 1½in taller; **wheelbase:** 7ft 7in (2.27m); **kerb weight:** (roadster) 2072lb (972kg), (coupe) 2442lb (1110kg) add 12lb/5kg for V8 and 405lb/150kg for MGC; **wheels:** 14in (MGB), 15in (MGC); **turning circle:** 34ft 2in (10.2m); **fuel capacity:** 10 gallons/45 litres (roadster), 12 gallons/54 litres (coupe); **boot capacity:** 3½ft^3 roadster, 9ft^3 GT.
TECHNICAL: Engine types: 1798cc four-cylinder and 3528cc V8 (MGB), 2912cc six-cylinder (MGC), all petrol; **gearbox:** four-speed manual plus overdrive standard on later cars; **suspension:** (front) independent coil springs and wishbones, (rear) live axle, semi elliptic leaf springs; **brakes:** disc front and drum rear.
TRIM: Cloth, leather/leathercloth, last models were striped cloth.
KEY OPTIONAL EXTRAS: Works glass-fibre roof from 1963. White wall tyres, heater (on early cars), wire wheels, SP41 tyres, three-speed Borg-Warner 35 automatic transmission (1965-1973), Laycock electronic overdrive (standard fitment from June 1975), rear seating to make 2+2 for the roadster, inertia reel seat belts, popular aftermarket was the Webasto sliding fabric sunroof on the GT models, boot rack on roadster, Triplex heated rear window collapsible steering column from 1972.

For the 1973 model year, the five drilled holes on each of the three spokes of the steering wheel were replaced by single slats as seen here. Note also the adoption of sleeving on the gear lever. In all, four types of steering wheel were used throughout the B's life.

LATER MIDGET SERIES

Looking at the roots of the 1961-1979 MG Midget, the story starts with the charming Austin-Healey Sprite, affectionately known as the 'Frogeye' in the UK and 'Bugeye' in the USA, as the vehicle would always bring a smile particularly to young children with its frog-like front end. BMC launched the original Mk1 Sprite in Monte-Carlo, two days after the Monaco Grand Prix in May of 1958. Design had been undertaken by the Donald Healey Motor Company, and it was manufactured alongside Magnettes and MGAs in the Abingdon facility.

The Sprite Mk1 was originally offered at just £669, and production costs were kept down by using as many off-the-shelf parts as was possible. The bonnet was a front hinged affair that lifted forward complete with the front wings, similar to the Herald and later Spitfires from Triumph. For power, if you can call it that, the little 43hp A-series 948cc engine, borrowed from the Morris Minor and Austin A35, fitted the bill perfectly. Overall nearly 49,000 Frogeye Sprites were made to Mk1 specification. The vehicle's chassis design was the world's first high volume sports car to use unitary construction, with rear suspension featuring quarter-elliptic leaf springs, and front suspension by coil springs and wishbones. Cross-ply tyres were fitted to 13in wheels. A national sell-out week at the end of production proved just how popular the Frogeye was, with dealerships completely empty of Sprites by the end.

A splendid early Midget pleases the crowds at Helmingham Hall.
Below: The same Midget from the rear.

The MG Midget story commences with the introduction of the heavily revised Mk2 Sprite in May 1961. These new cars were virtually identical, save for the MG's chrome side trim, a different grille, and obvious badging differences. The prices were as follows: Austin-Healey Sprite base model £660, the Sprite deluxe £675, and MG Midget £689. The base model Sprite was available for home markets and lacked windscreen washers, rev counter, a fixed passenger seat and had absolutely no bumpers. It is unknown if any examples of this model were actually sold!

To separate the cars, the Midget launch followed that of the new Sprite in June 1961. These cars are now affectionately known as 'Spridgets'. The higher cost of the Midget was justified by extra instrumentation and better trim, including more piping on the seats. All cars had Perspex side-screens at this point and no wind-down windows. The name Midget

An early production Midget interior.

Immaculate instrument panel of a very early Midget.

was familiar to MG enthusiasts, having been used on the M-Type, D-Type, J-Type and T-series of cars in the past. Between 1961 and 1970, Innocenti built its 950 Spider which used Spridget running gear, but was styled by Ghia.

With the introduction of the Midget and Sprite Mk2 in 1961, still with the old 948cc engine in both, larger 1¼in SU carburettors were now fitted, and the bodywork was completely refreshed particularly at the front and rear. The rear wheelarches were lowered, now covering more of the wheels and tyres, this feature giving the rear end more strength. There was now actually a locking boot lid (it was previously a scramble to get access to the 11½ft³ stowage area from behind the seats with the Frogeye, the rear end being engineered to give the bodyshell more rigidity), and thus now there was a conventional rear bumper. Headlamps were re-sited into a more modern position at the front corners of the front wings, which themselves no longer opened with the bonnet panel.

Performance was never startling, road testers of the time achieving around 87mph top speed with a 0-60mph time of approximately 18 seconds. There was a no-fuss two-spoke black steering wheel and the small rear-view mirror was placed in the middle of the metal dash top. Instrumentation was by Jaeger, and was unique to the Mk1 Midget. Three Midgets were prepared as works entries in the November 1961 RAC rally; only half of the competing cars finished

A 1965 Midget follows an Austin A40 into an Ipswich classic car event.

1960s interior.

base model Sprite was deleted from the price lists and brochures. Jack Brabham was by now installing the 1220cc Coventry Climax OHC engine into Midgets for £360. The Brabham-Midget was tested by the well-known John Bolster of *Autosport* magazine. The power mill was 40lb lighter with an alloy head which helped improve performance. Reaching 60mph in nine seconds was a revelation, and the car's top speed was 107mph. Its test was titled "A really potent sports car with vast reserves of stamina ...". It could cruise at 90mph for ages, these were pre speed limit days for UK motorways of course. Speedwell provided another conversion with similar performance figures and also marketed sliding handles so that the doors could be opened from the outside on early cars.

due to arduous special stages, but the three Midgets all completed the route, one with wishbone damage and the other two took first and second place within their class. 16,080 Midgets were made with the smaller 948cc engine.

For the 1963 model year, both models were upgraded and utilised the more powerful 56hp 1098cc BMC (10CG) engine also seen in the latest Morris Minors, Austin A40 and BMC 1100s. 8½in disc brakes were fitted at the front replacing the earlier drum units, and, like the new MGB, wire wheels became optional and the steel units changed appearance slightly as they lost their circular perforations. At last carpets were fitted (albeit plain type and not flecked) in the front to replace the rather utilitarian rubber mats. The

The Mk2 MG Midget (and Mk3 Sprite), made its introduction in March of 1964. Now 1098cc (BMC code 10CC) strengthened engine block castings were adopted with changes to the crankshaft main bearings. Glass changes included a more pronounced curve to the windscreen, and the addition of quarterlight windows on the leading edges to the front doors. Door windows were now finally able to wind down. Another quick identity giveaway was that external door handles were fitted, no more leaning into the car to get the doors open. Suspension changes included the adoption of proper semi-elliptic rear springs to replace the quarter-elliptic variants previously, this gave

A 1968 1275 Midget.

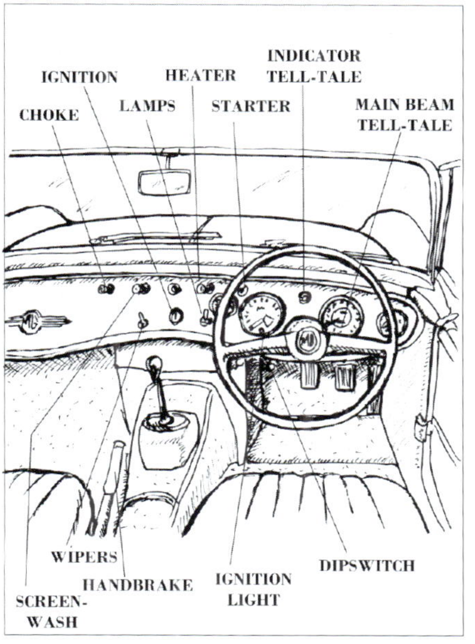

Above: 1971 Midget instrumentation. Right: Early dashboard layout diagram.

additional axle location. 25,905 Austin-Healey Sprite Mk3s were manufactured along with 22,601 Mk2 Midgets.

In Sweden in June 1965, Roger Moore who played Simon Templar in TV's *The Saint*, gave away a new car to the winner of the Stockholm beauty contest: not a Volvo P1800 as you might expect, but a brand new MG Midget. Fashion model Christina Leander was the lucky lady.

The October 1966 Motor Show held at Earls Court, London, was the platform used to launch the Mk3 Midget (and confusingly the Mk4 Sprite on the Austin-Healey stand). Up to this point the whole programme had been very successful, with over 160,000 Sprites and Midgets being produced, 73 percent of them exported. The all-singing, all-dancing Austin and Morris Cooper S Minis by now had the zestful and charming sounding 1275cc A series engine fitted, but MG enthusiasts were saddened to hear that the new Midget was fitted with a lower tuned version (65bhp vs 76bhp) and with a reduced compression ratio (8.8:1 vs the Mini's 9.75:1). This was down to model range placement, the new Midget engine in fully tuned state would have been quicker than its more expensive MGB sister. This new adoption now gave the Midget a 95mph top speed.

Other worthwhile improvements included a permanently fixed hood, previous versions were taken off and stowed in the boot: it had been a real chore to deploy the roof in an emergency. An instant rain downpour meant stopping the car, putting the metal frame on first, then covering with the hood, with the strong possibility of getting drenched! The new tonneau was of a superior design, which made it much easier to deploy. A safety-driven update under the bonnet was the separation of the brake and clutch master cylinders. For the 1968 model year, US models had smog pumps fitted which took up some of the extra power to comply with local regulations. For 1967 season USA cars, padded dashboards with smaller main gauges were now fitted, similar to the MGB models, as were triple windscreen wipers and extra side marker lights.

Correct stainless steel window wipers, sadly not always seen on restored cars.

Later series grille and side badging.

Reclining seats came in 1969, and an alternator replaced the dynamo to improve the electrical performance, the car by now had become 'negative earth'. From chassis number 66236, the rear axle ratio was increased from 4.22:1 to 3.90:1, giving better fuel economy, the car being more long legged, but acceleration suffered a little.

British Leyland was the holding company from late 1969, and thus largely cosmetic alterations were made. Updates to the appearance included the commonality of the Sprite and Midget models with a new satin matt recessed front grille with extra chrome, steel wheels again, revised badging with British Leyland motifs on the wings, M-I-D-G-E-T (or S-P-R-I-T-E) badges at the bottom leading edges of the front wings and black sills (the division marked by a chrome strip). Bumpers were now of a slimmer profile, and rubber caps were placed on the overriders front and rear, like the MGB. At the rear there were now squared off tail-lights. Some cars were built with a matte black windscreen surround, but this proved unpopular and was soon deleted. Brighter colour options became available at this point. Inside the car, the seats were of a more attractive design and beige carpets replaced the previous black ones with certain paint colours. The Sprite was discontinued in 1971, with the last 1000 or so simply badged as the Austin Sprite, in order to save on paying royalties to the Donald Healey Motor Company.

Rear boot chrome rack with picnic hamper by the sea …

Turners Car Preparations Ltd of Bedford offered an interesting conversion in 1971. Its oddball vehicle had a 1600cc GT Ford Capri engine and gearbox fitted to a Midget, good for an extra 9mph top end speed compared to the 1275cc standard engine. Also in the £1166 price were Panhard rods, front anti-roll bars, a higher final drive, improved brake pads and a double size fuel tank.

Sadly the 1971 road test car driven by

Motor's Tony Dron has been untaxed since 1984, according to the DVLA website, so it probably hasn't survived. The test was favourable, and with 50 percent more power than the standard car, the Turner's Car Preparations Midget was very pleasing to drive, apart from the fact that it overheated a fair bit. The magazine reported that driving it fast in bad weather was best, whilst listening to Led Zeppelin on the cassette machine at maximum volume.

Very late in 1971 (during the UK's K registration suffix) new Midgets left Abingdon with rounded out rear wheelarches, until late 1974 anyway, when the original shape returned. The rounded arches looked similar to the old Frogeye, but were now flared on the edges to strengthen the thinner metal. There was better heating, boot interior lights fitted, a bigger seven gallon fuel tank giving another 30 miles or so and a collapsible steering column. The power output for the North American specification cars dropped to 54½ hp.

A few months into 1974, like the MGB, the Midget saw the introduction of some rather ungainly bumper crash cans fitted for the USA market, these being fitted immediately before the last rubber bumper cars commenced. This was a very odd looking stop gap to get around the first of the new federal regulations in the USA.

Enter the so called 'soft-nosed' black rubber bumper models towards the end of 1974. These were styled to match the contours of the car and moulded from urethane foam over a steel armature base, with body structure improvements to strength to carry through any impact loads. Like the MGB, the ride height was raised so the car could comply with USA regulations, which affected handling, so to help get round this issue, anti-roll bars were added. The drive-line was completely refreshed: the engine was uprated at this point and the model was now known as the Midget 1500. Using a modified Morris Marina 1300 gearbox with full synchromesh and Triumph Spitfire 1493cc engine, power was increased to 65hp and sent to the rear axle through a single piece propeller shaft. The Triumph Spitfire was seen to be the Midget's closest rival, and if ever there was a comparison test published, ironically it was nearly always with this similarly-priced car.

Despite the extra 200lb in overall weight, the ripple effect here was that top speed was now 100mph, with a slightly better acceleration time of 0-60mph in 12 seconds. However, travel at top speed with the roof down and the drag co-efficient rate increases dramatically, so top speed drops to 94mph. On the downside there were 5in or so extra in length due to those big bumpers with no advantage to the passenger space. In 1976, US markets saw detuned examples of the Midget with just a single Zenith Stromberg 150 CD4T carburettor fitted. Overall power was down to 50hp, and just to confuse the Leyland Cars parts bin managers, squared off rear wheelarches were now fitted once more to help with the body strength. For reasons of vanity, the front wing arches were lowered to cover up suspension components made visible by the increased ride height.

The last mainstream road test was published in 1978 by *Autosport* magazine. For a model that was approaching 18 years

Canadian specification Midget 1500 with rubber bumpers.

Midget won praise: "… it did well, the latest Midget has a good performance – it's a genuine 100mph car – and as an open car for enjoying the fresh air it takes a lot of beating." To celebrate 11 years of Austin Healey Sprite and MG Midget production, the last 100 cars were all finished in black, with the final car completed on 7th December 1979. Of the rubber bumper 1500 models, 73,899 were produced in just over five years. The retail price by then had risen to £3821 and was listed into 1980.

The long production run of 17 years was summed up by *Autocar* in an early 1967 road test: "By regular power increases and trim changes, BMC have kept abreast of the trends; undoubtedly the MG Midget will be with us for some time yet." They were right! Many examples still survive today, and if you can cope with the seven gallon fuel tank, the very cramped interior with its decidedly tricky to get to door handles or fiddly roof deployment, they make a very interesting cheap classic car to run.

MG MIDGET BODY TYPE: Two-door roadster; **manufactured at:** Abingdon, and 476 at Cowley (early 1967), plus Australia as CKD kits; **approximate number produced:** 224,839 overall; **production span:** 1961-1979.

PERFORMANCE: Top speed: 80-100mph/130-160km/h (hood in upright position); **0-60mph/100km/h:** 14-17 seconds; **average economy:** 30mpg.

PRICE AT LAUNCH: £689.

MEASUREMENTS: Length: chrome bumper cars 11ft 4¼in (3.46m), rubber bumpers cars 11ft 9in (3.58m); **width:** 4ft 5in (1.35m); **height:** 4ft 1½in (1.26m); **wheelbase:** 6ft 8in (2.03m); **kerb weight:** (saloon) 1566lb (711kg); **wheels:** 13in; **turning circle:** 32ft 1½in (9.75m); **fuel capacity:** 6 then 7 gallons/27 then 33 litres; **boot capacity:** 11½ft^3.

TECHNICAL: Engine types: 948, 1098, 1275 and 1493cc four-cylinder petrol; **gearbox:** four-speed manual; **suspension:** (front) independent coil springs and wishbones, (rear) live axle, quarter then semi-elliptic springs; **brakes:** drum then disc front and drum rear.

TRIM: Leathercloth then PVC.

KEY OPTIONAL EXTRAS: Ace wheel trims on early cars, wing mirror, two hardtop types, tonneau cover, Ace Mercury wheel discs, white wall or heavy duty tyres, twin horns, rear compartment cushion, uprated alternator. The October 1973 introduced 'option pack' included a new tonneau and anti-roll bars.

1978 press advert for the rubber bumper Midget.

Speedo and rev counter of the Midget.

The 1975 model year Midget 1500 announced 16th October 1974. An unusual combination of spoked wheels and rubber bumpers on this early press car.

Midget media advertising slogans

Small wonder ...
She's inherited winning ways
Your mother wouldn't like it
Some day you'll settle down with a nice sensible girl ...
85% of MG Midget owners are men
You can do it in an MG
Sport the real thing. MG Midget
Go fly a Midget (USA)
Tyres gripping ... wheels humming, driving urge to master the miles with a come-on-let's-go roar
MG Midget blows your mind but not your budget (USA)
On the road, a sports car. In your budget, an economy car. (USA)
It can put you out in front. Without setting you back. (USA)
It's a lot of sports car for a little price (USA)
The air bites shrewdly
Our slung-low sweet chariots now come with button-down tops a 1275cc kick and anchors to match!
MG Midget adds FPG to your MPG. (USA)
Fun per gallon
MG Midget. High flying fun. Low flying price tag. (USA)
MG Midget. Heavy on the fun, Light on the budget. (USA).

THE MG METRO SERIES

Before any press announcements, Longbridge MG Metro production started in March 1982 to allow a build up for potential sales after the official launch in October 1982. Around 1400 cars were delivered to UK dealerships to match the anticipated demand. Following on after a ten-year gap since the demise of the MG1300, and a three year gap in seeing anything with an octagon badge since Abingdon closed, MG badged cars were front-wheel drive cars again, using the (camshaft uprated) A-series 1275cc engine, now with 100mph capabilities. Indeed this was the first 'straight from the factory' ton up Metro. Its mainstream rival had to be the Ford Fiesta XR2 which was some £350 dearer.

Two years prior to this, Austin Morris used the UK Motor Show as the platform to launch the new Austin Metro, a stylish three-door small car of 11ft 2in length with high lift tailgate, front-wheel drive and Hydragas suspension. In line with modern cars, the rear seating could be folded down (split 35/65 percent), to increase the modest boot-space from 7.5 to a cavernous 45ft^3, with the rear shelf removed and clipped out of harm's way for tall objects.

Early dashboard of the MG Metro.

Advertising comparing the base model with MG Metro.

The model range was from a rather bland base model (with vinyl seating and two black and unsightly rubber bungs on the tailgate covering up holes for the rear wash wipe on more upmarket models), then the Metro L décor (slightly better but with no frills), through to 1.3S, HLE and plush HLS. The general consensus of opinion was that this three-door super-mini was to replace the 21-year-old Mini, but ironically it was outlasted by the Mini and axed in heavily reworked form in 1998, two years before the smaller car was deleted.

There was no sports model, and two engine options were available, 998cc and 1275cc. The Metro was a best seller for Austin Morris and then Austin Rover. As MG models were prepared, a very plush Vanden Plas Metro was also marketed. For clarity at this point, there were also some Morris-badged Metro vans too. The MG badged version enjoyed all these modifications plus had a colour coded front grille, and added a touch of glamour to the existing Metro range. Wide alloy wheels with low profile tyres, strobe body stripes, twin red lines above and below the front grille, a rear tailgate spoiler (now seen on the HLS too) and a bright interior including high back rear seats, the model was clearly aimed at the modern young customer in a hurry. The aforementioned rear spoiler reduced the drag coefficient from 0.41 to 0.39, whilst the front retained its bib spoiler.

What was certainly evident was that the design included as many MG badges on the car that could be made practically possible, both inside and out, some 11 at the author's last count, including the floor mats. MG purists' eyes would roll as they knew full well that this was the first new model since Abingdon abruptly shut not long before. However, the marketing blurb stated it was so "the driver did not forget the heritage in his hands." There were plenty of red reminders both on and in the car too. Red needle punched carpets and red piping on the seats were evident, the seats were finished in black cloth with a grey herringbone centre. Unsurprisingly the seat belts were red too, from the outset. If the optional sunroof was ordered, the grey PVC roof lining was replaced with a grey cloth material.

The fitment of wider alloy wheels with their low profile tyres and consequent wheel offset to widen the track gave quite an improvement to the handling over the 1.3S Metro. Surprisingly, the use of twin carburettors from the previous MG 1300 were ditched, in favour of a more efficient single SU HIF 44 unit with larger choke. The carburettor sat on a new water-heated aluminium inlet manifold that was designed to stabilise the temperature of the fuel/air mixture. A modified clutch was fitted to cope with the extra power. Essentially, the MG version was almost mechanically identical to the Austin Metro 1.3S, including suspension and brakes.

Magazine staff were eager to get their hands on the new model. Several magazines reported a top speed of well over 100mph, and an overall economy of over 35mpg. *Autocar* magazine was pleased with the car at launch, stating, "the MG Metro comes out as a cleverly assembled, good value package that offers just enough spirit to satisfy the tastes of its potential buyers without invoking the wrath of the insurance companies." Referring to decade-old advertising it continued, "You can do it in this MG without paying through the nose for it." Advertising was clever too. "Your best friend will hate you" was the main double page spread seen in the media, with a silver Metro parked high in the mountains, and listed were all its performance and power facts. All for £4799!

Hot on the heels of the normally aspirated Metro was the MG Metro Turbo, which was announced at UK Motor Show time, and utilised a Garrett AiResearch turbocharger. It

Early MG Metro publicity picture.

cost £851 more than the standard car, and Austin Rover geared up to build 10,000 a year in 1983. Sub ten-second 0-60mph times were recorded at MIRA, the motor industry's research ground, and top speed was up by 10mph to 112. Test cars from MIRA were driven so hard that new clutches had to be fitted before resale.

Wider brake discs were fitted along with new callipers, and, understandably, several modifications were made to the more powerful engine (up from 72bhp to 93bhp) including improved water passages around the valves and an air cooler fitted on one side of the copper radiator. Pistons were strengthened and the forged crankshaft was nitrated. Even the exhaust valves were sodium cooled and all the valves now had double springs. Turbo model specific identification details spotted on the exterior included an extra two central bonnet louvres, and a two tone colour scheme with darkened body sides on at the bottom.

The deep front spoiler continued around each corner to the wheelarch spats, with shaped inserts for added brake cooling. Inside the vehicle, the digital clock was re-sited to

A 1987 Turbo press photograph, note the large headrests.

the centre console, replaced by a snazzy LED turbo boost indicator sitting squarely within the rev counter. The speedometer range was increased to 130mph, and better stalk controls graced the steering column.

Rear side windows now finally swung open like 1960s Minis and two-door 1100s, and the heater had a side window demisting facility. An almost overlooked modification was the repositioning of the washer bottle, now carrying extra capacity for the spray-type headlamp washers. In the end, 21,968 MG Metro Turbos were manufactured between 1983 and 1989, including an all-white version with white bumpers, spoilers and wheel trims, plus glass sunroof bronze tinted windows and central locking.

Contemporary advertising mainly concentrated on how well the car was doing on the race track, with a "We race. You win" full page colour press advert depicting a standard Turbo model below a track-driven Unipart racer, and another sponsored by British Car Auctions. Other adverts concentrated on the model's performance and again on how well it was doing on the race track, particularly in the 1982 British Saloon Car Championship well before the Turbo was available. In service they proved a little noisy on the motorway, with radios being turned off at anything above 70mph due to high wind and engine noise. What was really needed was a fifth speed on the gearbox. Broken engine mounts were a common complaint on enthusiastically driven cars, as were dashboard rattles and clonks.

Model revisions were made across the entire Metro range for the 1985 model year including a five-door Metro (none were MGs however), refreshed front end styling and a completely new interior featuring a more up to date dashboard, now fully-ergonomic with a one piece moulding featuring Montego style instrumentation.

MG models had a colour coded front grille, and the red pinstripes above and below it were discarded. The body colour was extended onto the door mirrors and handles on Turbo models, which also featured a red transfer style badge on the nearside leading edge of the bonnet, and adopted grey, not black, lower side body features with revised Turbo graphics. A further extravagant design feature along

Detail badging on the front of the Turbo.

Detail badging on the rear of the Turbo.

these lines occurred a year later, when the redesigned seat facings of the Turbo featured rather ostentatious diagonal pinstriping with the Turbo graphic matching even more red pinstriping on the door cards. Make no mistake, Austin Rover wanted you to know you were in an MG!

The non-turbo MG Metro was last seen on the UK new price lists in 1990 after over 37,500 cars had been built. Since 1987, the wheels were reverted to steel type following

A 1986 non-Turbo MG Metro.

6R4 advertising like this was common in the mid-1980s.

MG Metro 6R4 on display at the Gaydon Heritage museum.

a facelift that included modifications to the interior and dashboard. After this point the only choice for a sporty Metro was to buy a Rover GTa which lasted in production until 1998 under the Rover name.

Metro 6R4

The space-frame MG Metro 6R4 may have resembled a Metro but it shared very few components with the original car. Based on a three-door shell, the 6R4 was built with glass reinforced plastic wheelarches and sills, plus air dam spoilers front and rear and an integral roll-cage. Austin Rover was keen to achieve international rallying success within the Group B sector, and successfully competed against the short wheelbase Audi Quattro Sport, Lancia Delta S4 and mid-engine Renault 5 Turbo. The 6R4 had the largest cubic capacity engine amongst its rallying competitors, and power, via a specially designed 2996cc V6 engine, was fed from the rear to four wheel drive via a five-speed gearbox. Not built for top end, which may have been 120mph or so, but acceleration, with a 0-60mph time of just 3.2 seconds. The author can verify the sheer thrill of the G force both forwards and sideways, having ridden as an impromptu helmet clad

An airborne 6R4 mid rally.

MG METRO BODY TYPES: Three-door hatchback; manufactured at Longbridge; **approximate number produced:** 120,206 plus 21,968 Turbo variants; **Production span:** 1982-1989.
PERFORMANCE: (Turbo) Top speed: 110 mph/km/h, 0-60mph/100km/h; 10.9 seconds; average economy: 32mpg.
PRICE AT LAUNCH: £4799.
MEASUREMENTS: Length: 11ft 2¼in (3.4m); **height:** 4ft 5½in (1.36m); **wheelbase:** 7ft 4½in (2.25m); **kerb weight:** 1826lb (828kg); **wheels:** 12in alloy (13in on turbo); **turning circle:** 35ft 3in (10.75m); **fuel capacity:** 7 gallons/31.8 litres; **boot capacity:** 45.7ft³, seats down.
TECHNICAL: Engine types: 1275cc four-cylinder petrol; **gearbox:** four-speed manual; **suspension:** (front) Hydragas with telescopic dampers, (rear) uprated Hydragas coil pre-load springs and anti-roll bar, independent trailing arms; **brakes:** disc front (ventilated on turbo models) and drum rear.
TRIM: Cloth, velour, tweed.
KEY OPTIONAL EXTRAS: Fog lamps, mud flaps, sunroof, tow bar, clear coat metallic or black paint and matching red safety belts in the rear.

passenger in a Mobil 1 Computervision rally 6R4 around the Castle Coombe track on a Group B test day in the early 1990s. We were initially on the tarmac admiring the 2½ turns lock to lock of the precise steering, then off it and onto the grass when the track ran out! As a photographer on the day, I was suitably impressed and very grateful of the opportunity. A Clubman specification was also offered with a still quick 0-60mph time of around 4½ seconds.

Officially the 6R4 was not added to the standard car price lists, but action photos added to the back sections of the sales catalogues would please the eyes of many fans. *Autosport* magazine was full of photos and race reports through the mid-1990s. 205 cars were built to exceed special homologation rules whereby 200 cars were required to have been completed, some being fitted with smaller 2.5-litre engines.

MG Metro media advertising slogans

Turbo. MG style
Driving is believing (Turbo)
We race, you win
Your best friend will hate you
Move over, or move out of the way 'White Hot (Metro Turbo)'
Turbo, MG style
Car of the Year (Austin advert but with MG 1300 Metro picture)
Move Over, or Move Out of the Way (Turbo with Rover SD1 Vitesse)

MG MAESTRO AND MONTEGO

Maestro

To start the MG Maestro story, we have to first look at the similar bodied Austin Maestro, which was marketed from 1983 as a direct replacement for the Austin Allegro. The Allegro had been built for around ten years in two-door, four-door and three-door estate forms, in a variety of guises from base models up to wood-veneer dashboard Vanden Plas types in true Austin Morris style badge engineering. Sometimes rather cruelly referred to as the 'all-rust-and-aggro' by the Leyland bashers, it may have looked odd, but it did sell nearly half a million units.

The Maestro, known as LM10 in its design period, was launched in 1983, as an attractive five-door 'bread and butter' hatchback using standard suspension, no Hydragas or Hydrolastic as in previous models. It was slightly bigger than the Allegro, and had a larger glass area, a big rear tailgate, and came only in a four-door bodyshell. Initially there were no diesels offered. At launch, the top of the range Austin was the Vanden Plas, which used the 1.6-litre R-series engine, and had the famous talking dashboard. Lesser models were available with 1.3-litre units and more basic trim. The talking dashboard is discussed in the Montego section below, but for clarity it is important to point out that it was not just the MG version that had this feature, with 15 different languages, but the Vanden Plas Maestro too. The model was an instant success, out of over 605,000 Maestros built in an 11-year production period, 1983 saw the best-selling year at over 101,000 cars in total.

The idea was that a top model MG Maestro would represent the sporty side of the line, but this model was rushed by the development engineers for a quick launch, thus the more eye-catching MG Maestro 1600 (with twin carburettors and bigger 14in wheels) was announced at exactly the same time as the Austins. This model output 103hp, and whilst it was faster than the cheaper models, there were problems that came back to haunt Austin Rover: the twin Weber carburettors played up, the engine often ran rough and it was problematic to restart after just a few minutes of standing idle. Just ask yourself, how

The MG Maestro and the talking dashboard …

often now do you see an MG Maestro 1600 at a classic car show? Just 2762 were produced. The interior was made to look more appealing, with a lot of red features, too many to list but include red pinstriping for the bumpers; the red safety belts were certainly a talking point.

After just a year, and following 2762 cars built, the carburettor MG Maestro 1600 was quietly discontinued, and just over a year later a fuel-injected MG Maestro was announced, with the bigger 2-litre O-series engine. Its performance was certainly better than its predecessor had given. Top speed was up from 110mph to 113mph, and acceleration

Early publicity picture of the 1600.

Mid-season MG Maestro 2-litre EFi.

from 0-60mph down from 9.6sec to around 8.5sec. There were several differences too: there were suspension and braking upgrades, the EFi had colour co-ordinated bumpers, grille and door handles, a better interior, plus bigger 15in alloy wheels. The talking dashboard had certainly encountered some issues. The digital dashboard readout seemed a little blocky (but then so were home computers at the time) and not a patch on the GM Astra and Senator/ Monza GSE unit from Vauxhall Opel also in the mid-1980s.

The fuel-injected Maestro soldiered on until the end of production, but the real news came in October 1988 when the all-singing, all-dancing Maestro MG Turbo was launched, shown as a star of the 1988 Birmingham Motor Show, and to be available from the following spring. Priced at £12,999, and about £2500 more than its injected sister car, the Turbo was certainly no slouch. "Faster than a Ferrari, a Porsche, a Lamborghini, a Lotus, an Aston ..." the three page magazine advertising boasted, references being made to a select few models from other exotic manufacturers. The truth was in the testing, and *Autocar & Motor* magazine attained an incredible 131mph top speed (one way, best of two was 129mph) on the Motor Industry Research Association's test ground in the Midlands. Acceleration was scorching, with a 0-60mph time of just 6.9 seconds, the fastest

"Just light the red touch paper" 2-litre advertising.

Maestro 2-litre EFi under test.

Maestro Turbo publicity picture.

production front wheel drive it had driven to date. It was pitched against other hot rival hatches in the market, namely the Peugeot 309 GTi, Ford Escort Mk4 RS Turbo, VW Golf GTi and Vauxhall Astra GTE 16v. Fuel economy suffered, the Turbo recording a lowly 20.1mpg, not helped by the tester's enthusiastic driving.

Out of 43,574 MG Maestros made, the way more expensive Turbo made up just one percent of total production, with only 505 cars sold. The popularity of this model is high, some beautiful examples survive and can sometimes be seen at the various classic car shows around the country. In reality, it was very, very seldom that you ever saw a new Maestro Turbo when they were current. Just ahead of the Turbo launch, the Maestro range went under a revamp programme, adopting the more pleasing to the eye style dashboard of the Montego. At least the garish red safety belts were no longer fitted. It also shared the body-coloured rear spoiler which was a much more chunky design top and bottom.

Apart from the engine differences, visual changes against the standard 2-litre included script style badging, wider tyres, a full lower bodypack that made the body seem lower to the ground, and inbuilt front driving lamps. On the technical side there was a close-ratio gearbox, as the brochure stated "quicker through the gate than the Derby favourite ...". In late 1988, the interior was also treated to a revamp, and the Turbo adopted this too.

The revised Maestro EFi and Turbo models continued on in parity until late 1991, leaving just the Maestro base models and van to soldier on to 1994, when the model range was effectively replaced by the new Rover 200 range.

MG Maestro media advertising slogans

Born to perform miracles
Red letters, performance figures
Now injected. With adrenalin
You asked for some superb cars. So we designed one
Just light the red touch paper!
The Golf GTi will be along in a second
MG Maestro 2.0 EFi. Fuel-injected performance
Faster than a Ferrari, a Porsche, a Lamborghini, a Lotus, an Aston... (Turbo)

Montego

The MG Montego was based on the standard model Austin Montego, and, like its predecessor the Morris Marina/Ital that lasted until the Montego was launched in 1984, was available in both saloon and estate form. The Marina name was used first, of course, before it was facelifted and relaunched as the Ital

MG Montego front aspect.

MG Montego rear aspect.

towards the end of production after a mild restyle, helped by Bertone in Italy. The Ital continued the saloon/estate format but did not have a coupé version like its predecessor mentioned earlier in this book, as the 1.8TC used the MGB running gear.

The Austin and MG Montegos were longer than their predecessors, and wider. Whilst the original Austin badge variant used three engines (then a later diesel), the MG only utilised the 2-litre O-series mill, the EFi version lasting the entire length of Montego production. The gearbox was supplied by Honda, and suspension was by MacPherson struts at the front and a semi-independent trailing arm/torsion beam set up at the back. Central locking was a handy standard fitment. The rear seat was split so golf clubs could be carried even with back seat passengers onboard, as was the increasing trend on saloon cars at the time. When starting up, drivers were greeted with a female voice stating "Your monitored functions are working normally". Often this computer and voice synthesis would give out erroneous facts or instructions – irritating, and not obvious how to turn it off. One story went that a brand new vehicle, either an MG Montego or Maestro, crashed and ended up completely ruined, upside down in a dyke, half in the water with the boot opened in the impact, in very flat Fenland Norfolk. As the owner scrambled desperately to get out and open the door, the voice stated "Your interior light is on, and fuel level is low." Fortunately there was an 'off' button for everyday use!

The advertising blurb stated that the Montego EFi was aimed at a particular type of person, the performance driver, perhaps not unlike the Fenland driver above. All the media advertising was heavily leaning on the speed and acceleration angle (115mph, 0-60mph in 8.9 sec), whilst reminding the potential customers that these cars had an onboard computer with LCD message display. Bodywork was usually in bright colours, window trims were blacked out, and there was a black boot spoiler mounted at the rear. Alloy wheels were standard. No MG estate versions were ever sold, the plush Austin Montego Vanden Plas estate took the top spot for the luggage carrier title. To this point there never had been an MG estate car, these were to come later.

Eighteen months later, the aforementioned Vanden Plas saloon and estate were announced at the same time as the Montego Turbo (and Rover 216 series), and the city advertising bill-boards were boasting about a new performance car that proclaimed to be the fastest production MG ever. This was the MG Montego Turbo, in blown guise and pre-dating the Maestro version by over four years. Under the bonnet the engine was fitted with a Garrett T3 turbocharger which gave a fairly high 10psi of boost. Compared to the standard engine, the compression ratio was dropped from 9:1

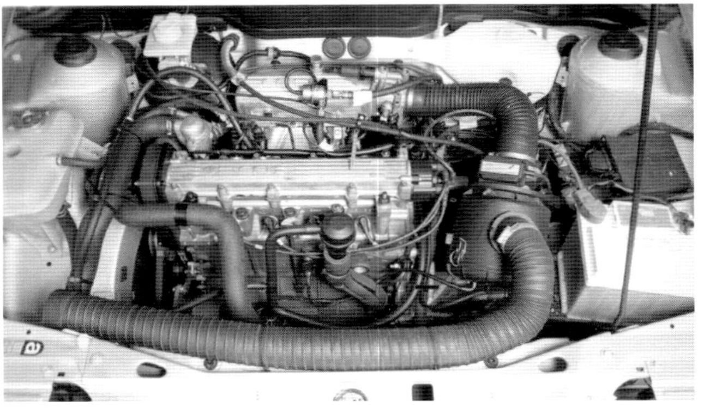

The 2-litre EFi engine.

Above: Montego advertising. "0-60mph in 8.9 seconds".
Below: Montego advertising. "0-60mph in 7.2 seconds", but mind the torque steer!

to 8.5:1 and apart from some minor changes, the engine was otherwise pretty standard. Overall there was an extra 33hp over the standard fuel-injected model, for an extra £2200. Surprisingly, the Turbo was not fuel-injected but normally aspirated with an ARG (nee SU) single carburettor, seen behind a multitude of intercooler pipes under the bonnet. For that you would get a set of Turbo graphics down each side too, if that was your cup of tea!

Other visual differences between the two models were a near-side red Turbo transfer on the leading edge of the bonnet, a front spoiler, wider rear boot spoiler and FM radio cassette as standard. Perhaps the computer dashboard had had its day as the instrumentation reverted back to standard format, and there was an extended centre console. Colour-keyed door mirrors were electrically heated and motion controlled, there were twin rear reading lamps plus a slide and

tilt sun-roof. Electronically lifting windows were now fitted to both the EFi and Turbo models. Performance was certainly stunning, advertised at 126mph and a 0-60mph acceleration time of 7.3 seconds.

Motor magazine reported in its April 6th 1985 issue report, "… the Turbo has a torque-steer problem of considerable dimensions." This comment continued that it mattered not that the road was wet or dry, and that, "Quite simply, under hard acceleration, whatever the gear, the Montego would rather go in any direction other than straight ahead." Clearly that kind of power was tricky with a front wheel drive! The factory was quick to get round this issue with revisions quickly made to mostly alleviate the torque steer. The suspension was hardened, bush rates were improved by hardening the rubber, and alterations were made to the steering, including fitting a ¾in bigger steering wheel while the ratio was changed from 2.8 to 3.3 turns lock-to-lock. It largely worked. These modifications allowed for less body roll, too.

In late 1988 the Montego range was improved, the new models being designated AR9. Improvements were made to the suspension for a smoother ride. The name Austin was phased out, and new models included a very economical diesel variant. The traditional Rover Viking badge was now present on the cars, but the word Rover was never seen. Trim improvements were made to the interior and dashboard.

Like the Maestros, all MG Montegos were phased out in late 1991, with Rover just producing the Montego estate in six forms from this point until 1994, to make way for the Rover 400. It would be a two year wait for the RV8 to see a return to the MG name in the new car catalogues.

The advert that stated the Turbo was the quickest production MG of all time.

The last prices on the UK market for MG Maestros and Montegos were:

MG Maestro 2.0 EFi
£12,910
MG Maestro Turbo
£14,299
MG Montego 2.0 EFi
£14,580
MG Montego Turbo
£15,705

MAESTRO AND MONTEGO BODY TYPES: Five-door hatchback (Maestro), four-door saloon (Montego); **manufactured at:** Cowley; **approximate number produced:** 43,574 plus 505 Turbo (Maestro); 37,476 plus 7276 Turbo (Montego); **production span:** 1983-1991 (Maestro); 1984-1991 (Montego).

PERFORMANCE:
1600 Maestro – Top speed:

110mph/ 175km/h; **0-60mph/100km/h:** 9.6 sec; **average economy:** 28mpg.
Maestro Turbo – Top speed: 131mph; **0-60mph/100km/h:** 6.9 sec;
Montego Turbo – Top speed: 126mph; **0-60mph/100km/h:** 7.3 sec.
PRICE AT LAUNCH: Maestro 1600 – £6245, Maestro Turbo – £12,999, Montego EFi – £8165, Montego Turbo – £11,397.
MAESTRO MEASUREMENTS: Length: 13ft 3¼in (4.05m); **width:** 5ft 6in (1.68m); **height:** 4ft 8½in (1.43m); **wheelbase:** 8ft 2½in (2.51m); **kerb weight:** 2190lb (993kg); **wheels:** 15in alloy; **turning circle:** 33ft 8in (10.31m); **fuel capacity:** 11 gallons/50 litres; **boot capacity:** 38.5ft^3, seats down.
MONTEGO MEASUREMENTS: Length: 14ft 8in (4.47m); **width:** 5ft 7in (1.71m); **height:** 4ft 8½in (1.43m); **wheelbase:** 8ft 5in (2.56m); **kerb weight:** 2190lb (993kg); **wheels:** 14in (1600) then 15in alloy; **turning circle:** 34ft 6in (10.5m); **fuel capacity:** 11 gallons/50 litres; **boot capacity:** 16.2ft^3.
TECHNICAL: Engine types: 1598 (early carburettor Maestro only) then 1994cc four-cylinder petrol; **gearbox:** five-speed manual (no auto option); **suspension:** (front) independent coil springs, (rear) coil springs; **brakes:** disc front and drum rear.
TRIM: Cloth/velvet.
KEY OPTIONAL EXTRAS: Sunroof, fog lights, light delay unit, roof rack, electric tailgate release, power steering.

Montego media advertising slogans

The quickest MG production car of all time (Turbo)
Montego Faster
The performance car that puts the driver first

Cutway illustration of the Montego Turbo.

MG RV8

At the time of writing, the cost of a British Motor Heritage shell for an MGB is about £17,000 with good availability. They have been manufactured since 1988 using the original factory press tooling that had been made redundant after 1980, but most of the 750 tools were kept during the intermediate years. Essentially, owners of rusty or damaged MGBs can strip out the vital components, and, after painting, can rebuild the car as new, with the option of fitting other new parts into the bargain. All this proves the popularity of the marque. It was no surprise that in mid-1991 pictures leaked out from the press of Rover's plans to produce a 3.9-litre car, to be slightly restyled but built on a British Motor Heritage MGB shell with revised panels for the following year, and planned to launch it at the Birmingham Motor Show. It would break the 12-year MG tradition of producing hatchbacks and saloons but no roadsters.

Following the Rover senior management meeting in the summer of 1989, and noting the worldwide sales success of the Mazda MX-5 two-seater sports car, 30 Rover Special Product engineers had started work on the RV8 concept in 1990. It had been proved that the modern fuel injection system could be used within the B shell as one of the three cars brought along for discussion purposes had been retro-fitted as such. As a point of interest, at the meeting there was also the first completed Heritage shell car, and the last of the line British Motor Heritage Trust bronze MGB roadster (already mentioned, that now resides in the Abingdon Museum).

Named Project Adder, the team used a rubber bumper shell as a start, and developed a more modern curvaceous look for the outer panels. The end result looks very pleasing, a kind of 'how it would have looked' if production had continued model. A smoothed-out bonnet power bulge, nothing like that of the MGC, was evident to clear necessary V8 fuel injection ancillaries, and the old style quarterlight windows were a thing of the past. The front and rear wings were widened to accommodate the extra track width, and wider wheels were fitted. There were brand new headlamp units and colour matched front and rear smoothed out bumpers. A limited slip differential was also added to deal with the extra power.

Rover was aiming for the MG RV8 to be on sale for £26,000, and using the trusty 190bhp 3.9-litre Range Rover fuel injected V8 engine. First it was proposed to build 1500 units, soon to be extended to 2000 (in the end it was actually 1983 units in total, not including

A dealership selling one of the pristine MGRs imported from Japan.

The very plush leather and wood interior of the RV8 was a far cry from the early vinyl MGB days of the early 1960s.

development cars) making use of the Rover SD1 LT77 five-speed manual gearbox along with a new Salisbury axle. The suspension and braking systems were reworked extensively, but the car still retained semi-elliptic leaf springs and uprated drum brakes at the rear. The front brakes were ventilated. Burr elm wood was painstakingly used to create the dashboard and door cards, whilst the seats were trimmed in beautiful Stone Beige Connolly leather. In addition, the door cards and pulls, dashboard, centre console, handbrake and gearstick all had the white stitched leather treatment. The dashboard dial surrounds were de-chromed, now VDO instrumentation (like TVR) with the outer edges finished in black. The whole interior appeared impressively luxurious, yet somehow still retained the feel and character of the earlier car, although (fortunately) a whole new heating system was utilised. A nice touch was the return to the old chocolate and cream theme to the front and rear badges, this theme was also carried over to the MG F.

A press release was sent out for 14th June 1992 publication. Following this, both the MG Owners' Club and MG Car Club were treated to an official pre-launch debut at Canley in the September, where enthusiasm was reported to be high.

The launch went ahead as planned at the 1992 UK Motor Show, and the reception was very good, with a Le Mans Green RV8 on display. £2500 deposits had already been taken from at least 250 customers by that point. UK's monthly magazine *Car*, November 1992 issue was already in print by the time the Birmingham Motor Show was opened and had emblazoned across the cover "We drive the new MG, world exclusive". Early production car K417DCY was driven in the UK's highlands, and an interesting fact was published. Steve Schiemmer, manager of Rover's Special Products Division informed us, "only 5 per cent of the RV8 is taken from the B. 20 per cent consists of retooled, re-sourced or modified components and the remaining 75 percent, amazingly, is completely new or drawn from other Rovers." The test RV8 was not fully mechanically finished, but Rover's development test mule, an old roadster

Rear aspect of the RV8.

registered TAD 92W with all the correct running gear, was sampled alongside. Production started in March 1993, the bodyshell was assembled at British Motor Heritage factory at Faringdon (18 miles south west of Oxford), and the shells then transported to Cowley to be painted and carefully hand completed at a rate of 15 units per week. The completed cars were all fitted with either a black mohair manually folding hood and were available in the following colours:

Standard colour options:
British Racing Green (metallic)
Black (non-metallic)
Flame Red (non-metallic)
Caribbean Blue (Pearlescent)
Nightfire Red (Pearlescent)
Flame Red (non-metallic)
White Gold (metallic, two variations)
Special order paint (extra cost):
Woodcote Green (Pearlescent)
Le Mans Green (Pearlescent)
Oxford Blue (Pearlescent)
Old English White (non-metallic)

The least produced colour was Old English White, just five units built (two were exported), whilst the most popular was Woodcote Green, with 1269 units built, but only five of these were originally registered in the UK, which saw 139 examples registered for the home market. Note, development cars are not

Top to bottom: The beautiful moulding of the rear bumper for the light, unique to the RV8.

R-O-V-E-R chrome badging seen on the front wings (Japanese export).

A return to the red and beige MG front badge for the RV8 in 1992. This style was also extended to the centre of the wheels.

Right: Beautifully kept interior displaying the original leather gear knob – many get replaced to the wooden type over the years.

An early RV8 on display in 2024.

included in this data. Once complete, each car was comprehensively road tested before either being sent to the dealer (or exported via Southampton docks, shipment started in January 1994 with the first 46 RV8s). All cars built were right-hand drive.

Seven months after the public debut in Birmingham, and following the start of production in March 1993, *Autocar & Motor*, UK's leading weekly motoring magazine, published a comprehensive eight page road test of the RV8, using one of three UK validation models registered K12MGR. Basic cost was £26,030 and they praised the strong engine, build quality, and found it pleasantly quaint. Against it they remarked that it had poor handling and had an unrefined and rather lumpy ride. "Simply put, and no-one argues the point, it is not a modern car but a modern interpretation which was born 31 years ago". The performance was as predicted, a 0-60mph time of just 6.9 seconds, and top speed of 136mph. This car, K12 MGR, was first registered in April 1993, had also made appearances in *The Sunday Times* newspaper,

Japanese imported RV8s had grilles for the air conditioning, as seen here, instead of fog lamps.

The thick rim steering wheel of the RV8.

plus *What Car?*, *Performance Car* and *Classic Cars* magazines. It still survives with a low mileage.

Most of the RV8s built were exported to Japan (another right-hand drive country) following a sensational debut at its October 1993 Motor Show, where it was shown in Woodcote Green which became a popular colour there, and created quite a buzz. Rover had hoped to sell 500 units in Japan, but in reality the number was much higher, with 1000 cleared deposits left by customers by the end of the event. Many have made their way back to the UK via a specialist dealer network following Japan's stringent government tests on older cars in subsequent years, and can be easily identified by the air conditioning system which restricts the passenger compartment a little, and R-O-V-E-R badges on the front wings. The air conditioning unit was a Japan-only fitment that added 30kg to the weight of the vehicle, and spot lamps were deleted at the front to allow room for the condensing unit.

A sprinkling of 91 cars were delivered into Europe during 1994 and 1995 and four models went to Australia. The last car built was completed on 22nd November 1995.

Footnote: Whilst compiling this book, somebody asked me to compare the handling of the MG RV8 to my old 1982 Triumph TR8 roadster with similar sized tyres. There is no comparison in any way shape or form, and more importantly, the RV8 successfully goes round corners in the wet!

MG RV8 BODY TYPE: Two-door roadster; **manufactured at:** Cowley (body shell initially prepared by British Motor Heritage at Faringdon); **approximate number produced:** 1983, plus prototypes and development vehicles, 1568 were originally exported; **production span:** 1993-1995.
PERFORMANCE: Top speed: 135mph/215km/h; **0-60mph/100km/h:** 6.9 seconds; average economy: 26mpg.
PRICE AT LAUNCH: £26,030.
MEASUREMENTS: Length: 13ft 1¼in (4.01m); **width:** 6ft 8½ in (1.69m); **height:** 4ft 4in (1.32m); **wheelbase:** 8ft 6½in (2.6m); **kerb weight:** 2427lb (1101kg); **wheels:** 15in alloy; **turning circle:** 34ft 1in (10.4m); **fuel capacity:** 11.2 gallons/51 litres; **boot dimensions:** 3ft 1in (0.93m) wide (max).
TECHNICAL: Engine types: 3946cc V8 petrol (Fuel injection); **gearbox:** five-speed manual; **suspension:** (front) double wishbones, anti-roll bar, (rear) live axle, leaf springs, anti-roll bar; **brakes:** ventilated disc front and drum rear.
TRIM: Leather.
KEY OPTIONAL EXTRAS: CD player (£590).

RV8 media advertising slogans

The marque has returned (brochure)
The shape of things to come (brochure)
The Marque has returned (Dutch press advert)

Note: no UK adverts found in magazines

MG F AND TF

On the first anniversary of the launch viewing of the MG RV8 at the UK Motor Show, the press was already leaking stories about a new MG Midget design for 1995. Plenty of sketched ideas abounded in the press; none hit the mark of what was to come, although it was certain that it would be a two-seater open car with soft top, codenamed PR3, and a rival to the new Mazda MX-5 and Lotus Elan. One key design idea was that it was not to have the fiddly soft top fastenings visible on the outside of the car. The proposed K-series engine was to be mounted centrally and transverse behind the passenger compartment, and many Metro parts would make the project successful. Other than the aforementioned MX-5 and Elan models, other forthcoming rivals would be the BMW Z3 and Fiat Barchetta. Further scoop photographs of a cleverly cloaked prototype appeared in March and April 1995, revealing that the name of the new model was to be the MG F. K-series engines were fitted to Metro mule-cars/vans and were often seen under test on roads in the Midlands.

Above and below: A 2001 MG F.

MG F

Enter a new dawn. Launched later in the year at the Geneva Motor Show, at last here was the first genuine new MG sports car for 33 years after the closure of the Abingdon plant. The end result was a 1073kg, 12ft 10in long, 5ft 10in wide, 4ft 1½in high, rear-wheel drive, economical sports car of modern appearance that would easily fit in a domestic garage.

The MG F had several design features of the 1985 longer EXE show car, including the aerodynamic style at the rear end. Air vents for the engine were neatly sculptured into the panel between the door and rear wheel, the stylish chrome and black screw-off fuel filler cap featured Allen bolts (these were for show only), and six-spoke alloy wheels were standard. Two models were available from the outset, both 1.8-litre, the standard MG F and the Variable Valve Control VVC £2400 with 'electrically assisted' steering (fewer turns lock-to-lock), ABS and half-leather trim. Hydragas suspension was used, with telescopic dampers and anti-roll bars all round. Performance was commendable with top speed between 116 and 137mph, and acceleration 0-60mph in 9.5-6.9 seconds, model dependent. There was no stowage area

An early publicity picture of the F.

The mid-1980s EXE concept car inspired the rear styling for the F.

upfront, this crash crumple-zone was reserved for the vertically mounted spare wheel plus brake servo and master cylinder. In April 1996, *Autocar* performed a triple road test between a VVC, Alfa Romeo Spider and BMW Z3. The decision of the best car was a close one, and in the end the cheapest (and fastest at 131mph) won: "But the MG F is the better car. It has a sharpness and composure about its handling that gets better as the speed rises, a refined ride, a punchy and characterful engine and a prettily unique profile. And heritage."

The first major modification occurred in 1997 with the introduction of a new hood and hardtop, and the option of leather seats was offered. Larger 16in alloy wheels could also be specified. In 1998, the 1.8i standard model received electric steering. The Abingdon limited edition was offered in the following specification: Brooklands Green paintwork with a beige Sonnenland leather interior and beige hood, wooden gear knob, a chrome pack and those 16in wheels. The steering wheel also had matching beige inserts, whilst the dashboard was enhanced with white dials on the instrumentation and wood trim.

The supercharged £29,500 Cheetah was revealed at the Geneva Motor Show and marketed from 1998 by an enterprising Rover dealership, its marketing material compared the reworked model to the 1934 supercharged MG K3. Intake air was fed via a Rotrex compressor that had been developed by Turbo Technics. Maximum power was 210 PS at 7000rpm, and supplier SP Components quoted a 150mph top end and a stunning 0-60mph time of 5.5 seconds, but this was never quite matched by the motoring press. The brakes were understandably reworked somewhat. It was available in four bespoke pearlescent colours: Cheetah Green, Cheetah Blue, Cheetah Yellow and Cheetah Red. Unique styling included a reworked front bumper integrating front splitter and enlarged cooling apertures to increase the air flow into the radiators. 17in wheels sat under wheelarch eyebrows on all four corners between which there was a one piece side moulding for each sill. Even the rear bumper was treated to a Nascar style cut-out with separate rear diffuser! An aircraft quality stainless steel exhaust came with a ten-year warranty, and optional green instrumentation dials came with yellow script and needle, and a pair of Cheetah eyes were backlit from behind the rev counter. There were many lookalikes that appeared, but nothing quite matched the original's quality ...

In 1999, the 75 LE was offered to celebrate 75 years of MG. It was black and red with a contrasting hood, leather interior, subtle use of chrome again and 16in alloys. The model 2000 phase two version was launched in September 1999 with several overall improvements and the addition of a body-coloured windscreen surround and model year 2000 revised centre console. A lighter walnut wood trim replaced the darker black ash type and the fuel tank was now double skinned. Indicator lens appearance changed, with a smoked effect replacing the previous orange units.

A year 2000 CVT (Continuously Variable Transmission) version was offered on the 1.8i. Still quite nimble, but not Ferrari-like, the CVT gave the car performance figures of 0-60mph in around 10 seconds and top speed of 118mph. This gearbox had its very early roots in Dutch Daf cars of the 1960s,

Another MG F publicity photo.

and was developed with ZFST of Belgium. MG called it the Steptronic option (later Stepspeed), the cost was £17,995 and it included a six-speed paddle shift. There were three driving modes available: Standard Drive selected continuously variable ratios keeping the engine revs to below 4500rpm, Sport mode allowed the engine to rev up to peak power at 5500rpm, and Manual mode allowed the driver to select from the six-speed set ratios either by a console gear lever or switches on the steering wheel, supercar style! Double-page press adverts proclaimed: "Look at it one way and it's a 6-speed manual." Then upside down at the bottom of the advert "Look at it another way and it's an automatic," and a mirror image car was shown underneath, upside down. Sadly, the cost was around 15 per cent more fuel burnt. Other manufacturers also adopted this gearbox, including the Fiat Punto and Nissan Almera models. It was not adopted for use with the VVC, as this model had failed new emission tests so was not a viable proposition.

A Wedgwood SE model was produced in blue with leather interior, CD player chrome trim and attractive 16in multi-spoke wheels with, for the first time, a boot spoiler. In 2001 the collectable Trophy 160 SE model came with lowered body, firmer Hydragas suspension, prominent rear spoiler, lowered and reworked front spoiler, 11-spoke alloys, AP bigger racing brakes with four pistons and 158bhp. 2000 bright yellow examples cars were produced, identified by a small Trophy 160 motif under the left hand tear

This immaculate 27-year-old MG F is owned by the author's neighbour Jeff, and was one owner from new when he purchased it in 2015.

The interior is completely original with unused cigar lighter and ashtray, the odometer reads just 26,338 miles, Jeff calls it a real keeper!

tail-lamp. Cost: £20,995. Also in 2001, a lower specification 1.6i joined the range, as did the Freestyle SE, a VVC with Trophy body and wheels. The MG F was replaced in 2002 by the restyled TF. In all, 77,269 Fs were sold between 1995 and 2002. A one-off XPower 500 F was made in 2002, featuring a Garrett turbocharger and many body modifications. Plans were looked at to extend this to the TF but never materialised.

Buying used? There have been many horror stories bandied about of premature head gasket failure on higher mileage cars, and the same with the 1.8 K-series Land Rover Freelander too. It is always worth checking the dipstick for signs of any coolant ingress, and making sure the system has the correct pink anti-freeze present. VVC cars are identified by a plenum chamber under the bonnet and a letter T for the eighth letter on the VIN plate (the 1.8i is a G).

TF

In 2002, the TF115 (1.6-litre at £15,750), TF120 (Stepspeed at £18,245), TF135 (1.8-litre at £17,245) and TF160 range topper (£19,995) replaced the earlier MG F model. Its opposition was strong, the new Vauxhall VX220 and Toyota MR2 were snapping at the heels of the MG F. Over the F model, there were aerodynamic changes to the body shape and entirely new coil spring suspension fitted giving the vehicle a lower stance. In particular the rear was heavily reworked, with new trailing and track control arms. A new style front grille was fitted. There were a greater choice of internal and external colours, as well as hood colour options. Different seat and door fabric was announced, and the K-series engine was of higher performance, increasing from 120PS to 135PS. When tested, the TF 135 achieved 127mph top speed and a 0-60mph acceleration time of 7.2 seconds. Useful for fast night driving, the headlamps incorporated projector and direction indicator

The TF 80th Anniversary model.

lamps. MG stated that the body was 20 percent stronger than its predecessor, helped by a new one-piece side pressing.

For the 2005 model year, revisions included a glass rear window to replace the previous Perspex unit that fogged over time, and the TF135 received a new alloy wheel design. The suspension was also softened: 20 per cent at the front and 30 per cent at the rear. Inside the car, a facility was built in to see the heater controls in the dark, and Alcantara trim was now standard fitment, as were the front fog lamps. At last, a low coolant level light was standard on the dashboard. Design of the bumpers changed leaving a more pleasing line between the black section and the body colour, and the feeble standard single horn fitted to the TF was replaced with a stronger twin horn, like that used on the earlier F.

Fun advertising for the LE 500.

After around 600 2005 model year examples were manufactured, on 8th April 2005 the Rover factory closed after the MG Rover group collapsed, and that was the end of UK production. Ironically, the TF had been the UK's best-selling two-seater sports car, and plans were afoot to produce the TF GT version, but beyond a silver concept car with rare grenadine interior, this never came to fruition.

In 2007 Nanjing AC began its production in China. However, production arrangements were that the LE 500 was assembled in the UK at Longbridge, this was an improved limited edition of the TF135. The K-series engine fitted was now referred to as the N-series, and, fortunately, a stronger head gasket was installed from new. The motoring press were lukewarm about this model, not caring for the interior, which was now getting old fashioned.

The TF Sunstorm SE limited edition.

The 1.5 millionth MG to leave the production line was a TF.

Rear aspect of the TF.

"Undeniably flawed, but an appealing driver's car nonetheless" *Autocar* concluded in its 2008 road test. Specification included a body-coloured hardtop, air conditioning and rear parking sensors. In 2009 the TF135 was reintroduced with a lower starting price of £13,511. Finally, to celebrate the 85th anniversary of MG, a limited run of special model TFs was offered. They featured Bilstein dampers, thicker anti-roll bars and lowered ride height. New 'twisted pepper' style wheels from Rimstock were fitted, and three paint colours were listed as: Intense Cassis (aubergine), Ice White and Enigmatic Silver. An '85' figure was displayed in an octagon on the body sides with an unusual double stripe feature. The general consensus of opinion was that the revised suspension setup gave perhaps the best handling of any TF model.

MG F BODY TYPE: Two-door roadster; **manufactured at:** Coventry and Nanjing, China; **approximate number produced:** 77,269 (MG F), 39,249 (UK TFs); **production span:** 1995-2001 (MG F), 2002-2005 (MG TF), note Chinese production until 2011, some in Britain.
PERFORMANCE: Top speed: 125mph/200km/h; **0-60mph/100km/h:** 7.6 sec (7.2 sec for the TF 135); **average economy:** 31mpg.
PRICE AT LAUNCH: £15,995 (1995 MG F); £17,245 (2002 TF 135); £16,045 (2008 LF500).
MEASUREMENTS: Length: 12ft 10¼in (3.91m); **width:** 5ft 10in (1.78m); **height:** 4ft 1½in (1.26m), note TF 20mm wider and 30mm longer); **wheelbase:** 7ft 9½in (2.37m); **kerb weight:** 2466lb (1121kg); **wheels:** 15in/16in alloy; **turning circle:** 34ft 8in

The TF 135.

Interior of the TF 135.

(10.6m); **fuel capacity:** 11 gallons/50 litres; **boot capacity:** 210 litres.

TECHNICAL: Engine types: 1588 and 1796cc four-cylinder petrol; **gearbox:** five-speed or manual or continuously variable from 1999 (Steptronic six-speed); **suspension:** (front) Hydragas springs and wishbones, (rear) Hydragas springs; **brakes:** vented disc front and disc rear.

TRIM: Cloth or leather.

KEY OPTIONAL EXTRAS: Continuously Variable Transmission, metallic paint, hard top, body coloured hardtop from 2000, power hood, leather seats, RDS radio with CD player, bright finish ashtray, anti-lock brakes on earlier cars, optional three channel ABDS on TF, 16 in alloy wheels, passenger airbag, electronic steering, wind-stop, rear spoiler, exhaust finishers, headlamp protectors, moulded mudguards, Alcantara trim, foglamps and retro style luggage carrier. Grenadine interior on TF. Blue, grey and green coloured hoods were optional on the TF.

MG F/TF media advertising slogans

The drive of your life (brochure)
Typical. You spend £15,500 on a car and the roof comes off
£199 per month. Don't hang about
£199 per month. Yessss!
You can only do this with a great engine behind you. 9 inches behind you
Look at it one way and it's a six speed manual
Winter sports anyone?
Bought a sports car recently? Kept the receipt? (TF)
Before you know it, you'll be knocking on 60 (TF)
Fun is back (TF LE 1500)
Before you know it, you'll be knocking on 60 (TF)
Un mito che si scoprre, si copre e si riscopre. Sempre (Italy) (Translation: A myth that is discovered, covered up and rediscovered. All the time.)

TF Smokescreen interior.

This side shot of the TF at speed shows one of the side scoops that aids in engine cooling.

MG ZR, ZS AND ZT SERIES

The MG ZR, ZS and ZT bring up the rear of this book, as the last of the Longbridge MG saloons to be produced before the factory closed in April 2005. News of these new-to-MG models was scooped by the press in January 2001, describing them as extreme versions of Rover's range. The range even included diesels from 2002, a first for MG, plus the ZT-T estate car that, in modified form, broke a world speed record.

The MG ZR came in some pretty bright colours! Yellow was extremely popular.

ZR

The MG ZR was a popular three- or five-door sports hatchback based on the Rover 200 (later the 25), and quickly became one of MG Rover's quickest selling cars. Code named R3, the Rover 214 was launched in 1995 replacing the earlier 200 series. Main rivals at the time were the Ford Fiesta, Vauxhall Corsa and Astra. MG production started in 2001, about halfway through the production of the Rover 25. Both cars continued on until 2005 following a facelift (or Mk2 version) in 2004. Models were built alongside each other at Longbridge in Birmingham.

Four years ahead of anything badged MG, the Rover 200 was produced as a BRM derivative, first shown at the 1997 Frankfurt Motor Show. This was knocking on the door of the MG market, as it was a high specification limited edition car finished in Brooklands Green, its most distinctive feature was the adoption of an orange snout and exclusive woven mesh grille below the front bumper that was intended to be reminiscent of the old 1950s British Racing Green F1 race cars. Britain saw this model from 1998 and it is now collectable. The interior featured red leather quilted seats, plus plenty of red trim, belts and carpeting, a nod back to the earlier MG Metro and Maestros.

Management had noticed the interest in the Rover BRM, with its obvious connections to the livery of British Racing Motors in the 1950s. So, in 1999, when the Rover 200 was facelifted, it was named the 25, and it was this very model that the MG ZR was based on. The ZR supported a number of modifications made against the Rover badged cars, including performance and exhaust upgrades, uprated suspension, and interior modifications. "The Chilli Chewing, Pumped Up, Spine Tingling MG ZR" stated the advert headlines. Whilst the Rover 25 was equipped with five different engines (1.1-litre K-series, 1.4-litre K-series, 1.6-litre K-series and 1.8-litre K-series four-cylinder petrol units plus a 2.0-litre L-series turbo diesel), the MG version had the same choice, but no 1.6-litre or small 1.1-litre derivatives. The entry level was the ZR105, and the faster ZR120 had a top speed of nearly 120mph and sub nine seconds 0-60mph acceleration time. Solid disc brakes were fitted at the rear, and the range topping ZR160

The only commercial MG? The ZR was available as a van called the Express.

Later model ZR with the new corporate grille.

was even faster with vented front discs and larger rear disc brakes than its stablemates, with 131mph achievable. This top model featured special ZR 160 badges above a Union Jack and Chequered race-style finish flags. Two diesel variants were also marketed, badged ZR TD 100 (99hp), and a ZR TD 115 with engine adjustments allowing for a top speed of 116mph. *Autocar* magazine, entitled its launch article "These MGs transform the bland Rovers." All models came with a remarkably high rear spoiler.

There had been a Rover 25 style van, and, amazingly, the MG Express van (with the same footprint) became an interesting alternative to Corsas and Escort vans on the streets making light deliveries. For heavy payloads,

The ZR Trophy.

the loadspace at the rear was reinforced, and the rear side windows were replaced by bonded metal, which made the shell stronger. There were no rear seats, and in front of the bulkhead, the cabin was trimmed as a standard MG ZR. A total number of 317 were built and there was even a 101ps diesel version.

The 2004 facelift included new front and rear bumpers, rear tailgate and the headlamps were refreshed. Soft touch buttons were fitted to a new style dashboard, and the whole interior was revised. The Trophy model featured a sunroof, 'grid spoke' 16in alloy wheels, rear bumper extensions and a side sill and new rear light clusters. The top Trophy SE had all of this, but with 17in alloys (the 'straight' type) and no sunroof, but came with air conditioning.

BODY TYPES ZR: Three- and five-door hatchback (plus panel van); **manufactured at:** Longbridge; **approximate number produced:** 74,136 plus 317 vans; **production span:** 2001-2005.
PERFORMANCE: (ZR 160) **Top speed:** 130mph/210km/h; **0-60mph/100km/h:** 7.8 seconds; **average economy:** 35mpg.
PRICE AT LAUNCH: £14,345 (ZR 160 in 2001).

MEASUREMENTS: Length: 13ft 1¼in (3.97m); **width:** 6ft 6¾in (1.69m); **height:** 4ft 7½in (1.41m); **wheelbase:** 8ft 2½in (2.5m); **kerb weight:** 2403lb (1090kg); **wheels:** 17in alloy; **turning circle:** 32ft 8in (10m); **fuel capacity:** 11 gallons/50 litres; **boot capacity:** 10.7ft^3.
TECHNICAL: Engine types: 1396 and 1796cc four-cylinder petrol; 1994cc four-cylinder diesel; **gearbox:** five-speed manual; **suspension:** (front) independent coil springs with MacPherson struts, (rear) torsion beams with coil springs; **brakes:** ventilated disc front and drum or disc rear (model dependent).
TRIM: Cloth, leather.
KEY OPTIONAL EXTRAS: Front fog lights, yellow inserts on seats, yellow MG ZR steering wheel, side skirts, sun roof, electric windows, air conditioning, rear parking sensors, rear headrests.

ZS

The MG ZS was based on the Rover 45 platform that entered the market as the Rover 400 series in 1995. The production life of the

The Z series advertising could never be accused of being boring!

M6 motorway patrol cars were bright yellow MG ZRs at one point in 2001.

MG ZS mirrored the ZR, being launched again in the summer of 2001. The Rover 45 was available as a three-box style four-door saloon or hatchback with 1.4-, 1.6- and 1.8-litre four-cylinder petrol engines plus a two-litre diesel. The MG ZS version was created quickly after BMW sold off Rover, V6 prototypes had already been built and luckily the idea went into production. The engine range was the same as the Rover, except that there was no diesel, but a V6 2.5-litre engine topped the range. Over and above the Rovers, the MGs were built with new bumpers, headlamps and revised design tailgate or boot lid, creating a noticeably different car, and they were available in a series of bright colours.

At the top of the ZS range was the ZS 180, available in either body type. It shared the same appeal as the ZR 160, and adopted a similar approach to its badging, including the flags once again. Sporty style spot lamps up front helped enhance its looks, and it came with 17in alloy wheels as standard. The price for the ZS 180 was £15,995 and its top speed was 139mph. *Autocar* magazine described it as "extremely sorted" in their launch article and wrote: "Such infectious enjoyment in cars is clearly reflected in this very surprising and entertaining package."

After Chinese manufacturer Nanjing Automobile acquired the Longbridge plant, it displayed the ZS at the Shanghai Motor Show badged as an MG5 but it never made it into production.

BODY TYPES ZS: Four-door saloon, five-door hatchback; **manufactured at:** Longbridge; **approximate number produced:** 25,357; **production span:** 2001-2005.

More caffeine-fuelled advertising.

PERFORMANCE: (ZS 180) **Top speed:** 139mph/225km/h; **0-60mph/100km/h:** 7.2 seconds; **average economy:** 30mpg.
PRICE AT LAUNCH: £17,295 (ZS 180 in 2004).
MEASUREMENTS: Length: 14ft 9in (4.54m); **width:** 6ft 3¾in (1.92m); **height:** 4ft 6½in (1.39m); **wheelbase:** 8ft 7½in (2.62m); **kerb weight:** 2833lb (1285kg); **wheels:** 17in alloy; **turning circle:** 32ft 8in (10m); **fuel capacity:** 12 gallons/55 litres; **boot capacity:** 370 litres.
TECHNICAL: Engine types: 1.4 (Ireland & Portugal), 1.6, 1.8 (four-cylinder) and 2.5-litre V6 petrol, plus 2.0 turbo diesel; **gearbox:** five-speed manual; **suspension:** (front) double wishbone coil springs, (rear) anti-roll bar, coil springs; **brakes:** ventilated disc front and disc rear.
TRIM: Cloth, leather.
KEY OPTIONAL EXTRAS: Cruise control, leather trim, rear spoiler, airbags, alarm, leather seats (model dependent).

ZT and ZT-T

Codenamed Project R40, the Rover 75 model adopted the classical look, which still looks stunning today in both saloon and (from 2001) estate form. The car took its name from the old Rover 75 P4, a quality car launched a few years after the Second World War that lasted for a long time in various guises and was, and is still, highly respected. With the modern alternative's long 2.75m wheelbase, it was certainly a head turner with initially three engine options, followed later by the 4.6-ltre V8. Perhaps its main rival was the locally produced Jaguar X-Type 2.5, although this was nearly £3000 dearer. Gearboxes were the Getrag 283 five-speed manual or the five-speed Jatco JF506E automatic, at least until the V8 arrived. The large front wheel drive Rover 75 was debuted at the Birmingham Motor Show in October 1998 with sales following from June 1999. In 2002, the Rover was also offered as a special long wheelbase car and badged as a Vanden Plas. After this, as initially displayed at the Geneva Motor Show in 2004, the rear wheel drive V8 version was introduced with reworked front styling.

Thus, the final of the trio of new saloon cars launched in the summer of 2001 was the mighty MG ZT, this being based on the Rover 75 discussed above. The marketing

The ZT 260 V8 SE with Monogram Aurora paint finish.

The Mk1 ZT 1.8T.

department were soon to compare it to the BMW 5-series: "So much for the ultimate driving machine! Eight out of 10 people preferred driving the MG ZT." During the development of this car, the codename adopted was X10 and X11 (saloon and estate). Noticeable changes to wheel and tyres from the 75 gave the MG badged-version a different identity and the revised front bumper included the MG front grille. A chrome waist-line was placed down each side. New instrument faces and revised dashboard treatment was evident. Just one trim level was available, although a 'plus pack' could be added. The estate model was known as the MG ZT-T and advertising for it included the title "The Non-Organic, High Cholesterol, Maximum Strength MG ZT-T". The ZT 180 Auto was available from early 2002, and two-litre diesel models followed a few months later. Advertising headlines for the ZT 190 read "The Fire Breathing, Full Bodied, Red Blooded MG ZT."

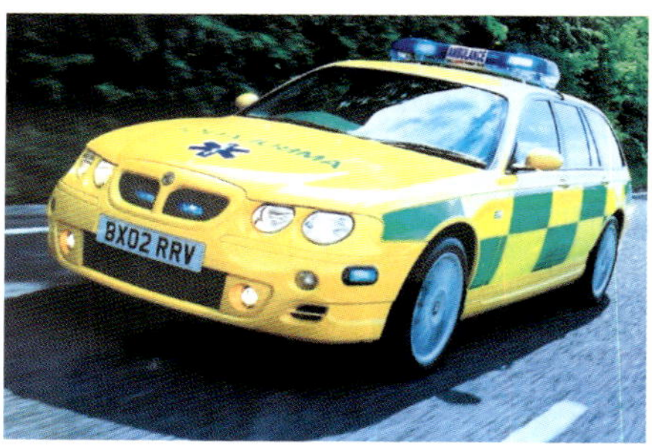

A ZT-T ambulance, the West Midlands & Shropshire Rapid Response vehicle.

The Extreme XPower 500 prototype certainly made the headlines in 2001 after its first promotional appearance at the Le Mans circuit that summer. Based on a ZT and finished in a lurid green with grey base, this was a forerunner to the V8 version available sometime later. So powerful, it would spit flames out of the twin exhausts when changing down gears, this one-off car would top 190mph on the track with an acceleration time of 0-60mph in 4.5 seconds, 0-100mph in 8.4 seconds. The gearbox was a six-speed manual Tremac linked to a Hydratrak limited slip differential and the power sent on to huge 18in wheels. Up front was the now familiar Ford-sourced all alloy 4.6-litre V8, coming in at 500bhp.

In July 2003, the 1.8-litre 120 model became available, and 160 models were built with a turbocharger. The following September the MG ZT-T became the world's fastest production estate car, where it achieved 225.6mph taking part in the Bonneville Speed Week Nationals on the Utah Salt Flats in the USA. It was Mobil 1 sponsored and heavily modified with an upgraded 800bhp Roush V8 engine.

At UK Motor Show time in 2003, the 260 V8 version was launched which gave some pretty amazing performance figures. Top speed was limited to 155mph, whilst 0-60mph acceleration times were down to 6.2 seconds. This was a very low volume car, with the estate model even rarer. A major difference was the use of a stronger Ford Mustang four-speed automatic gearbox to handle the extra power.

The press had been loaned some early cars, and the press pack stated "The more you drive it, the more you appreciate its unique

Rear aspect of the ZT-T.

Footballer Robbie Savage collects his new ZT from Terry Hunt, General Sales Manager of MG Rover Group.

This specially modified ZT-T topped 225mph at the Bonneville Speed Week.

'muscle-car' character that flies in the face of our competitors' trend towards buzzy high-revving engines."

More aesthetic changes were announced in early 2004 along with the Rover 75, the most noticeable was the deletion of twin headlamps and adoption of a single lamp unity either side of a fresh new grille. The rear changed too, there was badging placed below the number plate, plus a quicker steering rack was fitted. New instrumentation was fitted plus there were cosmetic changes to the seat cushions. Keen early buyers of the V8s already built were not happy that their new vehicles were to be obsolete stock within just a few weeks and the company had to adopt a strategy to deal with irate buyers. News had leaked out by way of incorrectly submitted advertising pictures in three newspapers that depicted the new frontal treatment far too early.

In 2006, a solitary ZT-T 385 that had been made for Rover management before the company collapse, and a supercharged assessment vehicle was released into the wild. With the same 4.6-litre V8 block, the car was good for 176mph and 0-60mph in just 4.7 seconds. Ironically, Ignition Blue BX54 KJE was probably the fastest MG ever built …

BODY TYPES ZT AND ZT-T: Four-door saloon, five-door estate; **manufactured at:** Longbridge; **approximate number produced:** 25,279 (and 883 V8s including Rover V8, 2003-05): **production span:** 2001-2005.
PERFORMANCE:
2.5 V6: Top speed: 140mph/225km/h; **0-60mph/100km/h:** 7.8 seconds; **average economy:** 27mpg.
4.6 V8: Top speed: 155mph/250km/h (limited); **0-60mph/100km/h:** 6.2 seconds; **average economy:** 22mpg.
PRICE AT LAUNCH: £20,495; **V8** £27,995.
MEASUREMENTS: Length: 15ft 7in (4.75m) note estate is 2in longer; **width:** 5ft 10in (1.78m) **height:** 4ft 8in (1.42m); **wheelbase:** 12ft (2.74m); **kerb weight:** 3086-3649lb (1400-1655kg); **wheels:** 18in alloy; **turning circle:** 37ft 1in (11.4m); **fuel capacity:** 14.5 gallons/66 litres; **boot capacity:** 432 litres (saloon).
TECHNICAL: Engine types: 1.8 four-cylinder, 2497cc V6, 4600cc V8 petrol; **gearbox:** five-speed manual; **suspension:** (front) MacPherson struts coil springs and anti-roll bar, (rear) Z-axle multi-link coil springs; **brakes:** ventilated disc front and rear.
TRIM: Cloth, leather.
KEY OPTIONAL EXTRAS: Cruise control, leather/Alcantara trim, rear spoiler, airbags, alarm, leather seats (model dependent).

ZR, ZS, ZT media advertising slogans

The chilli chewing, pumped up, spine tingling MG ZR
The full fat, high caffeine, maximum strength MG ZR (and ZS/ZT)
The full on, high calorie, maximum strength MG ZR
If you're not a car enthusiast, this is hardcore porn (ZR)
Vous cherchez la gentille-voiture-bien-comme-il-faut? (France, ZR)
The genetically modified, testosterone fuelled, grin inducing MG ZS
The last time you had this much fun in a car you ended up a parent (ZS)

The XPower SV was produced in limited numbers.

The XPower SV-R.

The non-organic, high cholesterol, maximum MG ZT
The Fire Breathing, Full Bodied, Red Blooded MG ZT
So much for the ultimate driving machine (ZT v BMW)
And now the new MG ZT 120 from only £15,995
There are sports cars. And then there are sports cars (ZR, ZS, ZT)

SV and SV-R models

Between 2004 and 2005, the senior MG management developed a flagship for the MG line, with a retail price between £65,750 for the base model SV and up to £85,000 for the SV-R from the MG Rover Group from May 2004. These prices were set at the Geneva Motor Show in 2004, where many major companies' concept cars are displayed every year, along with specialist coachwork etc. The concept's history spread back over a decade and through two previous companies. Initially as the De Tomaso Bigua, then as the Qvale Mangusta. Qvale was bought out by MG in 2000, and so after four years of concepts, a total carbon-fibre reskin followed.

The models were packed full of technology and features, and had the revised 2004 front end from the other cars, plus very similar headlights to the Vauxhall Calibra. These were good looking V8 coupés, built with carbon-fibre bodywork on a lightweight steel chassis with full rollover protection to FIA standards. The chassis was manufactured not at Longbridge but in Italy, then production was completed in the UK.

The ZT's Ford 4.6-litre V8 engine was developed to produce 320bhp, and even larger 5.0-litre 380bhp versions were made. Most of the contemporary press activity states it was a fantastic car, but let down by its rather un-special interior. The SV-R soon followed, this model boasted 700bhp and the Club Sport version was priced at £82,950. A bigger Ford Mustang V8 engine was (4996cc) used and plans were for 240 builds per year and for MG to place it on the race track in the following year But due to the collapse of Rover, only about 50 completed models were made (it is rumoured that two of them were automatic) making these highly collectable.

This stunning SV-R now visits classic car shows in Suffolk, lovely registration number!

APPENDIX 1

Main MG TV and movie appearances

Most TV and film companies request vehicles from manufacturers for a long time, stating that the model's exposure will help advertise their project and hope the vehicle will be supplied free of charge. Apart from one or two notable exceptions, most of these MGs that have appeared on either the small or the silver screen are not factory registered, which is a bit of a giveaway that the film crew had tried with the factory and failed, or just sourced a vehicle locally.

Actors Claudia Cardinale and Darry Cowl with an MG TF Midget in 1960.

The complete list of course is endless – where does one stop? This section lists the cars that have appeared in either regular form on a long-standing TV show, or perhaps in a long scene in a TV series or film, such as a car chase for example. I have limited the list to English speaking films, but there are quite a few overseas entries that could have made this list, too. The list is very loosely in approximate car production date order. Most of the films are quite old, and it is good to see the models in correct trim and with the contemporary street furniture.

Have a look on imcdb.org for further makes, and you can even search by TV show or film name.

- J2 Midget – *The Gay Divorcee* (movie)
- K2 Magnette – *That Girl From Paris* (movie)
- PA Midget – *My Week with Marilyn* (movie)
- PA Midget – *Battle of Britain* (movie)
- PA Midget – *Poirot* (TV series)
- PA Midget – *The Ship that Died of Shame* (movie)
- SA 2-litre Tourer – *Rebecca* (movie [1940])
- SA 2-litre Tourer – *Cluny Brown* (movie)
- WA 2½-litre – *Penny & the Pownall Case* (movie)
- YA 1¼-litre – *The Iron Lady* (movie)
- YB 1¼-litre – *Ruth Rendell Mysteries* (TV series)
- TA Midget – *Blood from the Mummy's Tomb* (movie)
- TA Midget – *Heartbeat* (TV series)
- TA Midget – *Hi-de-Hi!* (TV series)
- TB Midget – *Gilda* (movie)
- TC Midget – *Oliver's Story* (movie)
- TC Midget – *The Body Said No* (movie)
- TC Midget – *Love Story* (movie)
- TC Midget – *All Creatures Great and Small* (TV series)
- TD Midget – *Heights of Danger* (movie)
- TD Midget – *Life at the Top* (movie)
- TD Midget – *Two for the Road* (movie)
- TD Midget – *Eight is Enough* (TV series)
- TF Midget – *Funny Farm* (movie)
- TF Midget – *The Famous Five* (TV series)
- Magnette ZA – *Vicious Circle* (movie)
- Magnette Varitone – *The Deadly Affair* (movie)
- Magnette III – *Night of the Prowler* (movie)
- 1100 – *Children of the Damned* (movie)
- 1100 – *The Baron* (TV series)
- MGA – *The Perfect Furlough* (movie)
- MGA – *Daughters of Satan* (movie)
- MGA – *Out of the Shadow* (movie)
- MGA – *Heartbeat* (TV series)

MGB GT – *Melys* (music video)
MGB – *The Ipcress File* (movie)
MGB – *The Champions* (TV series)
MGB – *The Adventurer* (TV series)
MGB – *The Peacemaker* (movie)
MGB – *The New Avengers* (TV series)
MGB – *The Uninvited* (TV series)
MGB – *Tango 2001* (movie)
MGB GT – *Birthday Girl* (movie)
MGB GT – *Strangers* (TV series)
MGC – *The Avengers* (TV series)
MGC – *Connecting Room* (movie)
Midget – *Fox* (movie)
Midget – *The Dick Emery Show* (TV series)
Midget – *Heartbeat* (TV series)
Midget – *That Kind of Girl* (movie)
Midget – *Please Sir!* (movie)
Midget – *Bergerac* (TV series)
Metro 6R4 – *The Winning Streak* (TV series)
Metro – *Howards' Way* (TV series)
RV8 – *Ruth Rendell Mysteries* (TV series)
RV8 – *Solitaire for 2* (movie)
MG F – *The Man Who Made Husbands Jealous* (movie)
MG F – *RPM* (movie)
MG F – *Jonathan Creek* (TV series)
MG TF – *Emmerdale Farm* (TV series)
MG TF – *Winter Solstice* (TV series)
ZR – *Spooks* (TV series)
ZS – *Waterloo Road* (TV series)

An MG Magnette.

APPENDIX 2

Main MG appearances in motorsport events

Many of the sportier MG cars have appeared in a variety of motor sport events since the 1920s, but MG saloons have also been entered into competitive events and some with successful results, either by private individuals, or by the works teams. There were many ZA and ZB Magnette saloons seen on the European rally scene, as well as unlikely entries with the little ADO16 1100/1300 series. Into the early 1980s, and Austin Rover entered the 1600 MG Maestro in Rallysprint track events, and in the late 1990s, the ZR and ZSs were a regular sight at several prestigious venues.

The C-Type of the Earl of March, 1931.

International class records

In addition to motor races and rallies, MGs have also been used in various land speed record events at Montlhéry, Pendine Sands, Brooklands banked circuit, Gyon, Frankfurt, Dessau, Jabbeke and Utah up to 1959 when any works funded entries ceased. Some notable International Class Records achieved are:

EX120 at Montlhéry, 103.1mph (Eyston, 1931)
EX127 at Montlhéry, 118.3mph (Eyston, 1932)
EX127 at Montlhéry, 120.5mph (Eyston, 1932)
EX127 at Montlhéry, 128.6mph (Denly, 1933)
EX135 at Montlhéry, 128.6mph (Eyston, 1934)
Gardner-MG at Dessau, 204.2mph (Gardner, 1939)
EX179 at Utah, 153.6mph (Eyston and Miles, 1954)
EX181 at Utah, 245.6mph (Moss, 1957)
EX181 at Utah, 254.9mph (Hill, 1959)
EXF at Utah, 217.4mph (1997)

The Earl of March racing team photographed in Dublin, 1931, for the International Grand Prix.

Racing driver George Eyston trying out an MG at Brooklands circuit.

Rallying

The first MG to win a gold medal was a K3 Magnette at the Land's End Trial back in 1925, and numerous cars won or were in the top few finishers throughout the 1930s, 1940s, and up to the 1980s. Many MGAs and MGBs were entered into gruelling European rallies including the Monte-Carlo, Circuit of Ireland Trial, Scottish, RAC, Coupe des Alpes, Tulip, Mille Miglia, Circuit of Mugello, Liège-Rome-Liège, Acropolis, Midnight Sun, Austrian Alpine, Targa Florio and the 84 Hours Marathon at Nürburgring. A specially lightened 200hp MGC (the very last of the Abingdon racing models) won its class at Sebring in 1968. Many privateers continued to represent MG in various rallies and events through the 1970s. In the USA the MGB brought many race successes in American Production Car racing. The MG Metro was a regular sight zipping about on the UK track during the early 1980s and cars were sponsored by Computervision, Canon, Unipart, British Car Auctions, and even *Autocar* magazine. By the mid-1980s, the Metro 6R4 was designed and built to compete in the World Rally Championship (often with Tony Pond at the wheel) in various Group B events against other strong works-entered cars.

Le Mans

MG has never won a Le Mans race outright, but there were some notable results at the 24 hour Le Mans event. Notably, three works MGA prototypes (EX182) were entered in the 1955 event that ended in tragedy for so many, including those in the crowd that lost their lives. Two of the MGs finished (12th) by Ken Miles and John Locket, and (17th) by Ted Lund and Hans Waeffler. The car of the unfortunate Dick Jacobs and Joe Flynn did not finish, after losing control, rolling, then ending upside-down and burning. Driver Jacobs survived with severe injuries, but he was never to race again. Notable results for MG include:

4th (1st in class) 1934, K3 Magnette
9th (1st in class), 1935, P-Type Midgets
2nd in class, Midget TC, 1950 (George Phillips and Eric Winterbottom)
Three works EX182s (MGA) competed, 1955
Class win and 12th, 1960, MGA (Ted Lund and Colin Escott)
Class win, 1963, MGB
Motor Trophy, 1964 (Paddy Hopkirk and Andrew Hedges) MGB
2nd in class, 11th overall, 1965, MGB

In 2001, MG built two MG-Lola EX257s to compete in the event.

MG EX127 at Montlhéry, France in 1931.

Other track events

Many circuits have hosted events where MG have successfully competed. Over the years, these included (this list is not exhaustive): Brooklands, Nürburgring, Donington Park, Montlhéry, Rand, Phoenix Park (Dublin), Palm Springs, Silverstone, Sebring, Goodwood, Snetterton, Riverside, Le Mans, Brands Hatch, Monza, Thruxton, Castle Combe, Cadwell Park and Oulton Park. A notable event was the Anglia Pheonix Championship in 1996 where an MGF took pole position in March of that year at Silverstone. Into the 2000s, and ZRs and ZSs took part in many BTCC events.

Ken Miles' famous MG R2 sits in the pits at Palm Springs, USA, 1955.

MGs on the track today

Following worldwide success of MGs in track events, today the MG Car Club offer enthusiasts track day experiences at a number of UK venues, where owners can take their own vehicle around the circuit at Goodwood, Silverstone, Cadwell Park, Snetterton, Castle Combe, Blyton Park, Anglesey or Donington Park. It certainly is a worthwhile experience driving your own car to its (and your own) limits without the worry of flashing blue lights appearing in the rear view mirror!

Team Atomic Kitten MG ZS EX259 Touring Car.

Below: MG cars drive from Brooklands to Brighton on the MG Regency Run in celebration of the marque's 80th Anniversary.

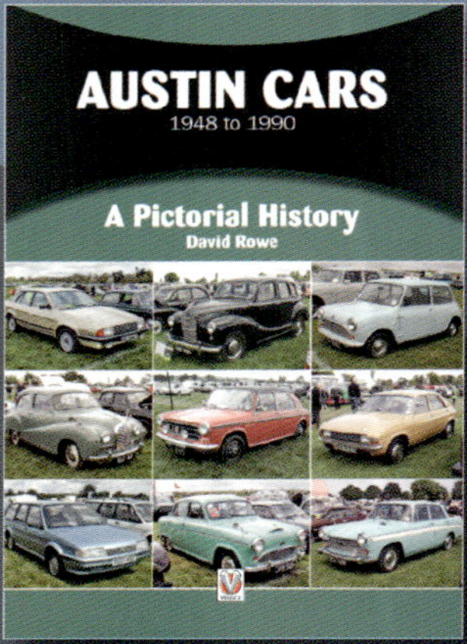

ISBN: 978-1-787112-19-3
Paperback • 21x14.8cm
• 112 pages • 275 colour and b&w pictures

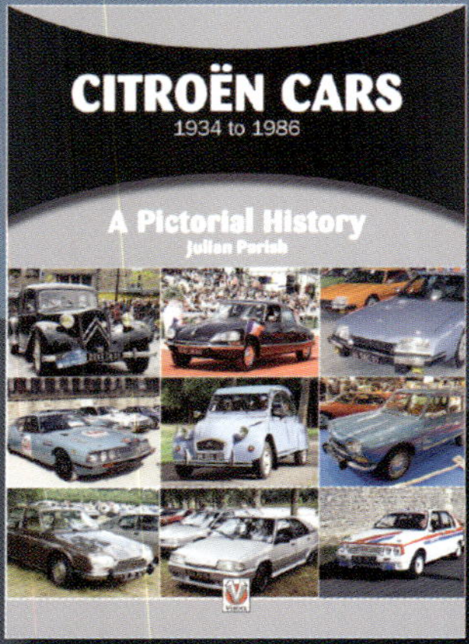

ISBN: 978-1-787116-36-8
Paperback • 21x14.8cm
• 152 pages • 350 pictures

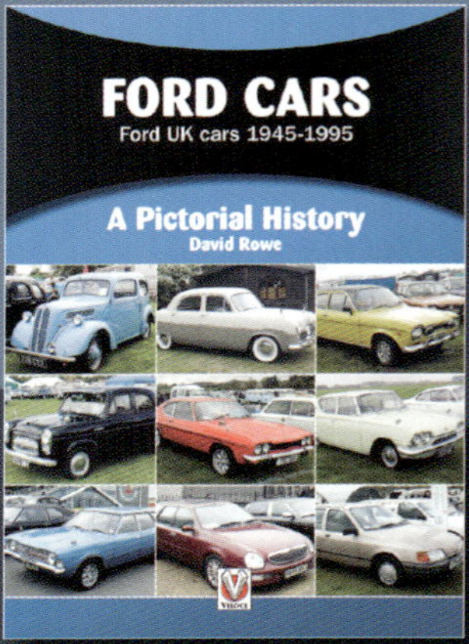

ISBN: 978-1-787116-42-9
Paperback • 21x14.8cm
• 160 pages • 330 pictures

A Pictorial History – the series

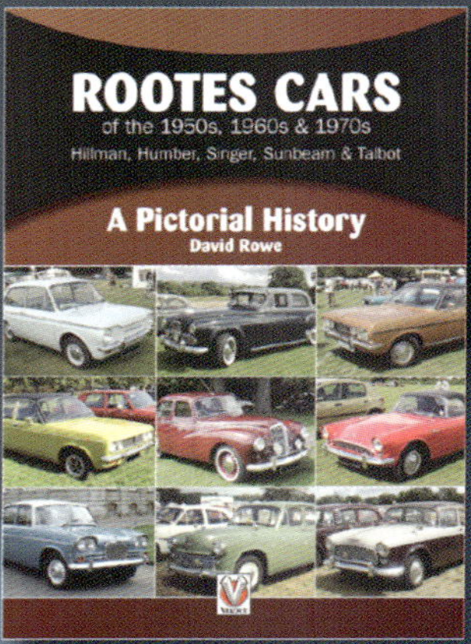

ISBN: 978-1-787114-43-2
Paperback • 21x14.8cm
• 168 pages • 1083 colour and b&w pictures

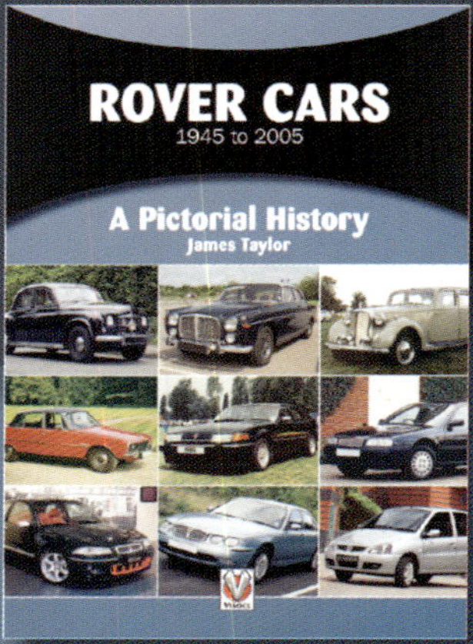

ISBN: 978-1-787116-09-2
Paperback • 21x14.8cm
• 80 pages • 300 pictures

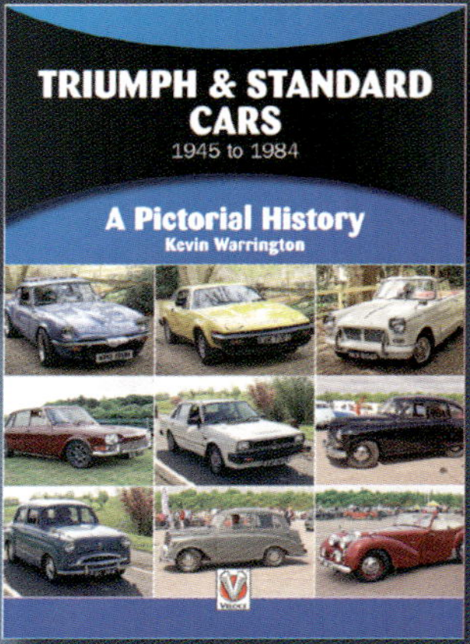

ISBN: 978-1-787110-77-9
Paperback • 21x14.8cm
• 96 pages • 244 colour pictures

More titles coming soon!

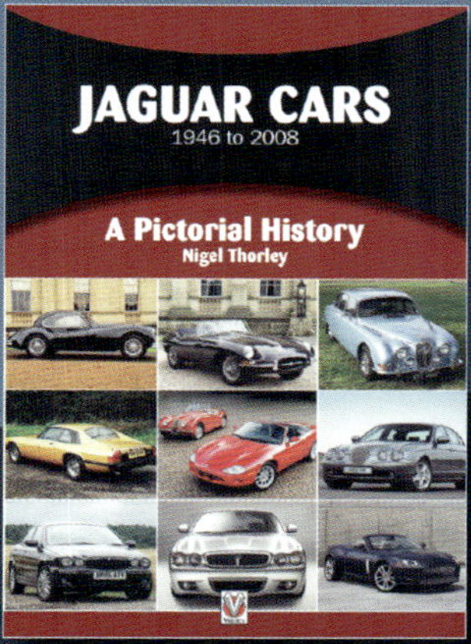

ISBN: 978-1-787117-76-1
Paperback • 21x14.8cm
• 160 pages • 387 colour and b&w pictures

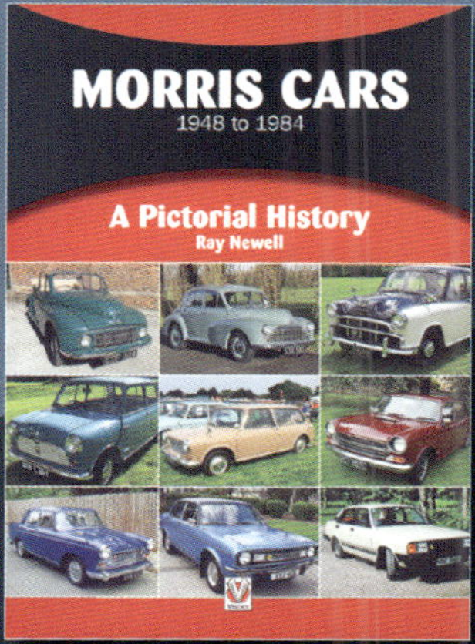

ISBN: 978-1-787110-55-7
Paperback • 21x14.8cm
• 144 pages • 425 colour pictures

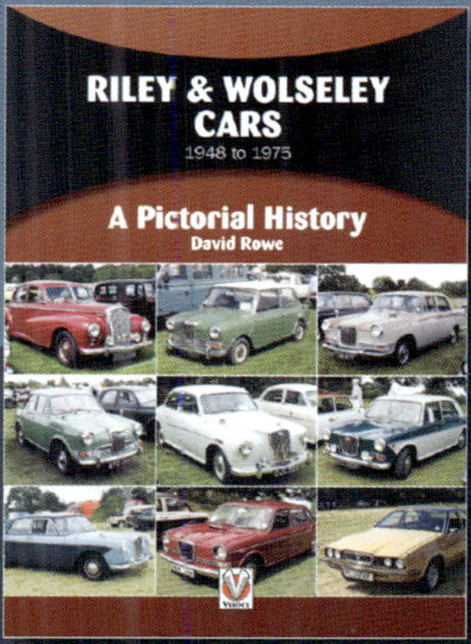

ISBN: 978-1-787117-91-4
Paperback • 21x14.8cm
• 104 pages • 352 colour and b&w pictures

These handy reference books cover all the key models, providing an overview of history and car design, detailed technical specifications and production data, all illustrated with hundreds of colour photographs and informative diagrams.

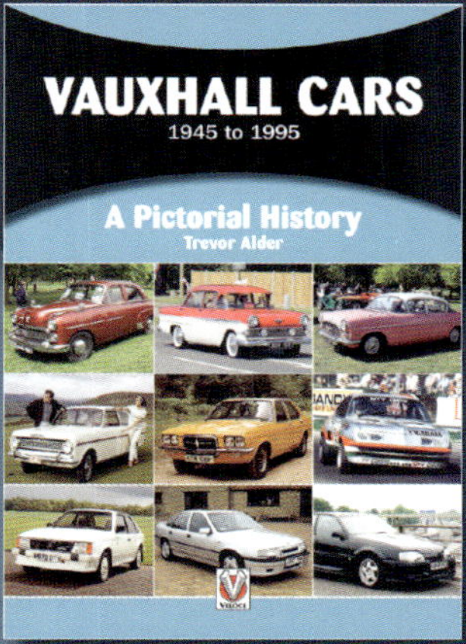

ISBN: 978-1-787115-93-4
Paperback • 21x14.8cm
• 160 pages • 339 pictures

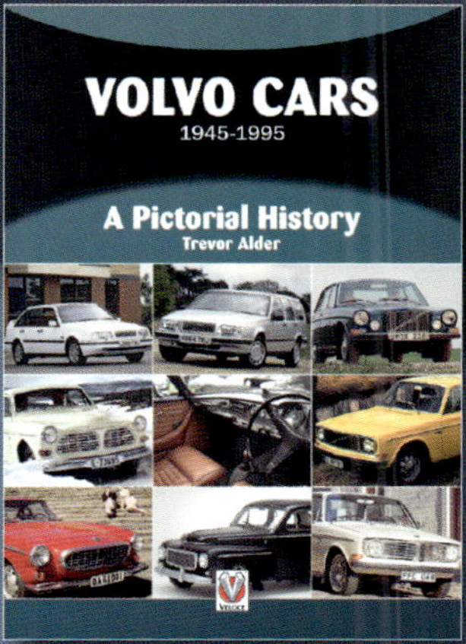

ISBN: 978-1-845846-13-8
Paperback • 21x14.8cm
• 112 pages • 216 pictures

ISBN: 978-1-845843-31-1
Paperback • 21x14.8cm
• 112 pages • 220 pictures

To see the full range of Pictorial Histories see www.veloce.co.uk

The Essential Buyer's Guide series

Having one of these books in your pocket is just like having a real marque expert by your side. Benefit from the authors' years of MG ownership, learn how to spot a bad car quickly, and how to assess a promising car like a professional. Get the right car at the right price!

Paperback • 19.5x13.9cm • 64-96 pages • circa 100 pictures

To see the full range of Essential Buyer's Guides, visit our website at www.veloce.co.uk • email: info@veloce.co.uk

INDEX

Model	Years of production	Page
TA Midget	1936-1939	15-21
TB Midget	1939	16-21
TC Midget	1945-1949	17-21
TD Midget	1949-1953	18-21
TF Midget	1953-1955	19-21
VA 1.5-litre	1937-1939	12-14
WA 2.5-litre	1938-1939	12-14
Y-Type 1.25-litre	1947-1953	22-25
ZA Magnette	1953-1956	26-30
ZB Magnette	1956-1958	28-30
ZR	2001-2005	96-98
Z	2001-2005S	98-99
ZT1	2001-2005	99-10
ZT-T	2001-2005	99-101